TABLE FOR 51

LESSONS LEARNED FROM SHARING MEALS ACROSS AMERICA

Praise for *Table for 51*

"Shari Leid's *Table for 51* is a testament to the power of face-to-face conversations in a time when too many people are hiding behind screens. Her courage to meet with strangers and acquaintances around the country also reminds us how every friendship starts as a connection with someone we barely know. Shari's story is the push we need to get out of our comfort zones and see the potential for friendship in unexpected interactions."

—Nina Badzin, Podcast: *Dear Nina—Conversations About Friendship*
DearNina.substack.com
Instagram/TikTok: @dearninafriendship
Facebook: Dear Nina: The Group

"*Table for 51* by Shari Leid takes readers on an inspiring journey through heartfelt conversations across America, where strangers become friends over shared meals. With each encounter, Leid, an Asian American woman, illuminates how our differences are often outweighed by our shared concerns and values, reminding us of our common humanity. This beautiful exploration is a testament to the power of connection and the importance of understanding one another."

—Dana Frank, National Bestselling Author
Get Up and Get On It: A Black Entrepreneur's Lessons on Creating Legacy & Wealth

"At a time when genuine communication and empathy is elusive, Shari Leid's incredible journey gives us all hope that human connection, no matter how difficult, is possible and can lead to major breakthroughs. *Table for 51* proves that when given the chance, everyone has a story to tell and when it's over a good meal, even better!"

—May Lee, Founder and CEO, Lotus Media House
Journalist, Author, Professor, Activist
www.lotusmediahouse.com
Email: may@lotusmediahouse.com
Instagram: @mayleeshow @shoesoffinsidemkt

"I wasn't sure what to expect from Shari Leid's latest book. I've read and loved all of her other ones and knew it would be a positive experience. She did not disappoint. She is such a beautiful soul who genuinely cares about other people and is gifted at building relationships. Connecting with fifty women, many of whom she had never met, takes courage—so does sharing her personal experiences. I am inspired by her and newly committed to connect with others."

—Keryl Pesce, Author, Entrepreneur
Co-host of award-winning "Happy Hour" on K104.7FM

TABLE FOR 51

LESSONS LEARNED FROM SHARING MEALS ACROSS AMERICA

SHARI LEID

Foreword by MIA BRABHAM NOLAN

Copyright © 2025 Shari Leid

All rights reserved. No part of this book may be used or reproduced in any manner without written permission from the author and publisher, except by reviewers, bloggers, or other individuals who may quote brief passages, as long as they are clearly credited to the author.

Neither the publisher nor the author is engaged in rendering professional advice or services to the individual reader. The ideas and suggestions contained in this book are not intended as a substitute for professional help. Neither the author nor the publisher shall be liable or responsible for any loss or damage allegedly arising from any information or suggestion in this book.

Capucia LLC
211 Pauline Drive #513
York, PA 17402
www.capuciapublishing.com
Send questions to: support@capuciapublishing.com

Paperback ISBN: 979-8-9915156-4-1
eBook ISBN: 979-8-9920502-0-2
Library of Congress Control Number: 2024926585

Cover Design: Ranilo Cabo
Layout: Ranilo Cabo
Author Photos: Wendy K. Yalom / www.WendyKYalom.com
Editing and Proofreading: Janis Hunt Johnson / Ask Janis LLC
Book Midwife: Carrie Jareed

Printed in the United States of America

Capucia LLC is proud to be a part of the Tree Neutral program. Tree Neutral offsets the number of trees consumed in the production and printing of this book by taking proactive steps such as planting trees in direct proportion to the number of trees used to print books. To learn more about Tree Neutral, please visit treeneutral.com.

Contents

Foreword		I
Author's Note		5
Dedication		7
Table for Two		11
Table 1	Albuquerque, New Mexico	
	Coffee with Nicole at Sawmill Market	17
Table 2	Honolulu, Oahu, Hawaii	
	Poolside Drinks and Bites with Nancy at Prince Waikiki Hotel	23
Table 3	Paradise Valley, Arizona	
	Lunch with Anna at Her Home	29
Table 4	Bal Harbour, Florida	
	Lunch with Paula at Le Zoo	35
Table 5	Las Vegas, Nevada	
	Lunch with Catherine at Mon Ami Gabi	45
Table 6	San José, California	
	Lunch with Hannah at La Terraza Grill & Bar	55
Table 7	Saint Charles, Missouri	
	Brunch with Brie at Prasino	59
Table 8	Austin, Texas	
	Happy Hour with Taylor at Kalimotxo	63

Table 9	Newberg, Oregon	
	Coffee with Traci at Chapters Books and Coffee	67
Table 10	Woodinville, Washington	
	Dinner with Tiernan at Heritage Restaurant|Bar	71
Table 11	Nashville, Tennessee	
	Lunch with Devin at Ella's on 2nd	77
Table 12	Johns Creek, Georgia	
	Brunch with Ashley at First Watch	81
Table 13	Huntsville, Alabama	
	Dinner with Laura at Purveyor	87
Table 14	Louisville, Kentucky	
	Dinner with Angie at Jeff Ruby's Steakhouse	93
Table 15	Greenfield, Indiana	
	Coffee with Kristin at Hitherto Coffee and Gaming Parlour	97
Table 16	New York City	
	Dinner with Mai Lara at Dons Bogam Wine Bar & BBQ	105
Table 17	Greenville, South Carolina	
	Dinner with Cindy at Halls Chophouse	109
Table 18	Goldsboro, North Carolina	
	Dinner with Melissa at The Laughing Owl	115
Table 19	Williamsburg, Virginia	
	Dinner with Megan at The Amber Ox Public House	119
Table 20	Eagan, Minnesota	
	Dinner with Ann at Ember & Ice, the Omni Viking Lakes Hotel	123
Table 21	Bismarck, North Dakota	
	Wine with Linda at Broadway Grill & Tavern	127
Table 22	Rapid City, South Dakota	
	Dinner with Toni at Her Home	131
Table 23	Oxford, Mississippi	
	Coffee with Keli at Heartbreak Coffee Roasters	135

Table 24	Bel Air, Maryland Brunch with Carrie at Barrett's on the Pike	141
Table 25	Millsboro, Delaware Dinner with Anne at the Clubhouse	147
Table 26	Phoenixville, Pennsylvania Wine and Cheese with Deardra at Vintner's Table	151
Table 27	Paterson, New Jersey Dinner with Talena at Hacienda	157
Table 28	Old Greenwich, Connecticut Sandwich Take-Out from Alpen Pantry with Kate	163
Table 29	Salt Lake City, Utah Lunch with Talar at The Copper Onion	167
Table 30	Cleveland, Ohio Brunch with Farrah at Astoria Cafe & Market	173
Table 31	Ann Arbor, Michigan Dinner with Angela at Seoul Garden	177
Table 32	Lansing, West Virginia Dinner with Twanna at Smokey's on the Gorge	181
Table 33	Palmer, Alaska Brunch with Noel at Turkey Red	187
Table 34	Denver, Colorado Dinner with Connie at True Food Kitchen, Cherry Creek North	193
Table 35	Casper, Wyoming Dinner with Barb at FireRock Steakhouse	197
Table 36	Little Rock, Arkansas Lunch with Lauren at Café Bossa Nova	201
Table 37	Great Falls, Montana Dinner with Rhonda at Her Home	205
Table 38	Moscow, Idaho Drinks at One World Café and Dinner at Lodgepole with Dana	211

Table 39	South Barrington, Illinois	
	Lunch with Judy at Apple Villa Pancake House	217
Table 40	Madison, Wisconsin	
	Dinner with Jennifer at Eno Vino Downtown Wine Bar and Bistro	223
Table 41	Davenport, Iowa	
	Dinner with Beverly at Duck City Bistro	227
Table 42	Cushing, Maine	
	Lunch with Cameron at Her Home	233
Table 43	Laconia, New Hampshire	
	Coffee with Emily at Wayfarer Coffee Roasters	239
Table 44	Randolph, Vermont	
	Dinner with Kristin at Kuya's at One Main	243
Table 45	New Orleans, Louisiana	
	Brunch with Allison at Flamingo A-Go-Go	247
Table 46	Boston, Massachusetts	
	Lunch with Tammy at Cheers on Beacon Street	251
Table 47	Newport, Rhode Island	
	Dinner with Sara at Brick Alley Pub & Restaurant	257
Table 48	Bartlesville, Oklahoma	
	Lunch with Janiece at Jude's Health & Java House	261
Table 49	Wichita, Kansas	
	Dinner with Jessica at Piatto Neapolitan Pizzeria	267
Table 50	Omaha, Nebraska	
	Coffee and Iced Tea with Sara at The Mill on Leavenworth	273
Table 51	Home	275
Epilogue		277
About the Author		279
Contact		281

Shari Leid, Author

January 1, **2024**

Dear Diary,

I refuse to be a secondary character in my own story.

Happy New Year,

Shari

Foreword

She doesn't know this, but one of the first emails I ever exchanged with Shari Leid lives on my desktop.

"I always have to remind myself that the past doesn't exist anymore and the future hasn't happened," she typed to me in New York City from Seattle, "so it is not real either. If I live in the past or worry about the future, I'm wasting my time on things that don't exist."

This email happened after I came across a snapshot of Shari from her fiftieth birthday party, in which she was sporting a pink mini-dress and her signature smile. I was intentionally internet-stalking her, preparing to write a story featuring her expertise. I went searching for more information on the cross-country, sit-down conversation project she'd told me she wanted to embark upon—which, unbeknownst to us both two years later, would become the book that is now in your hands.

I was instantly inspired by the picture she painted of her full embrace with life—by her. I had been struggling with the idealized version of my past self versus my current self. And here was Shari, celebrating everything she was, joyfully quoting Louise Hay: "I choose to make the rest of my life the best of my life." For me, it was both a warm hug and an electric shock that rattled me into the present.

She went on in that message to tell me another one of her favorite lines: "If today were the last day of your life, would you be doing what you are doing now?" *It keeps my energy where I want it to be,* she wrote. It was this question that changed her life—and she changed mine.

I was a relatively green writer, soaring and sometimes stumbling my way through the world of editorial. I had carved out a small space for myself by writing about something I cherished greatly and which I believed was not given enough merit or assistance: *friendship*. One day, thumbing through a reader's story about a tumultuous yet meaningful thirty-year friendship rekindled after a falling out, I was nearly brought to tears. The phrase immediately popped into my head like an incandescent light bulb: *Friendships are love stories too.*

This saying dug its way from my head into the deepest part of my heart, and soon developed into a full-blown friendship column. I would end up talking to people from all across the world about how they met a friend—they were old pals; they were roommates; they were classmates who hated one another at first; they found each other online; etc.—and about a struggle they were facing—one was moving away; just had a baby; was evolving in ways that made the other uncomfortable; they were starting to work together; they were moving in together; or they were taking their first trip together (*eek*)!

For so long, the media has told us countless romantic stories about a man and a woman falling in love, as well as dramatized tales of family dynamics. But what about *friends*? And more importantly—what about friends who were fighting, and drifting, and moving, and changing—and trying their best to stay in it together?

We're always seeing stories on how to get an ex back; how to find a new lover; what not to say in an argument with your partner; and how to help our significant other through a hard time. But where was a blueprint for platonic relationships? Where was the map for fostering meaningful connections later in life, for fighting to hold onto our friendships?

Friendships are relationships as much as any other bond—which means they are relationships in which we experience utter joy and complete turmoil as much as any other.

I wanted to do more than just tell stories about friendships. I wanted to help people who loved their friends and held them dearly, who wanted more than anything to figure out how to stay together—or to learn how to part amicably.

FOREWORD

So I asked.

I was led to Kat Vellos, a connection coach and the author of *We Should Get Together: The Secret to Cultivating Better Friendships* and of *Connected From Afar*. Then there was Danielle Bayard Jackson, a former teacher turned friendship expert who recently published *Fighting for Our Friendships*. I talked with people like Hannah Summerhill and Yseult P. Mukantabana, co-authors of the book *Real Friends Talk About Race*; licensed psychologist Dr. Marisa G. Franco, author of *Platonic: How the Science of Attachment Can Help You Make—and Keep—Friends*; and Buddhist meditation teacher Kate Johnson, author of *Radical Friendship*.

And then I met Shari Leid.

I first knew her as a former lawyer, friendship expert, and author. The first thing Shari taught me was that hearty conversations can lead to meaningful bonds, once and over time. She taught me, and all of my readers: to leverage awkward moments (like I would do when my braid got stuck in my purse zipper while meeting up with her); to get out of your head (lend a genuine compliment); and to strike up conversations that matter (over a meal is extra nice). She was able to do this because she taught it to herself.

When she turned fifty, Shari decided that she wanted to spend time engaging in richer discussions with people—from strangers to the people she knew best. She never felt like she was a natural at socializing, so she started with friends and women who lived near to her, which grew to dedicating a year to breaking bread with fifty women, many complete strangers, in all fifty states.

We would come to share many conversations like the ones with these women.

"Everyone we meet is both our teacher and our student." That's something Shari told me in our first interview. I immediately got the sense that she wasn't robotically networking, like so many people are, but seeking genuine connection. And at the table of life, which is already overflowing with bounty, she made me feel like she had room for me—and for anyone else, for that matter.

Many people feel that they grow into better versions of themselves as they get older. When I met Shari, though, I was feeling like I was going in the opposite direction. I was less patient and more angry than ever. I was less sure of myself and more pessimistic. Just two years after a global pandemic and a period of racial reckoning for many, I felt hopeless and divorced from any sense of togetherness and empathy—which I desperately craved. Shari Leid was the antidote.

She looks at every person not as a stranger, but as a friend she hasn't yet met. She doesn't run from awkwardness or rejection or discomfort; she faces and embraces it. She isn't afraid to let people in. She isn't scared to figure it out, and figure it out again. That alone is enough reason to read this book.

I wrote to Shari after seeing her fiftieth-birthday photo, and when I received her message back, I found myself excited for the first time in a long time. I found myself excited to grow older. Excited to dream. Excited to find new avenues. The past didn't exist anymore, in many ways. I didn't have to keep looking back. I could grow into the person I am today—and make it my favorite version of myself so far.

What this book represents is possibility: the chance to be ourselves and let others be themselves—without judgment. To listen and truly hear, and to speak and be heard. To grow, wildly. To support others. To witness, protect, and celebrate the humanity of the person across from us at the table—at any table. To peacefully coexist.

This book might as well be an extension of Shari. At the heart of this book *is* Shari. So at the heart of this book is love. May we all be students and teachers. May we all be heard, and may we all listen. May we all set the table for one more.

—Mia Brabham Nolan

Author's Note

Dear Reader,

I hope you're as excited as I am to come along on this incredible journey. As I sit here, surrounded by piles of paper and notes, giving my manuscript one last read, I can't help but look back on what's been an extraordinary adventure. When I first started out, my plan was simple: travel the country and meet fifty people—strangers or acquaintances whom I'd had little to no contact with over the past thirty-five to forty years. Little did I know, these individuals would become my teachers, sharing the wisdom of their life stories during our lively conversations.

Life, as it turns out, is full of surprises. From the moment I dreamed up this project to now, as I'm packing up my house and saying goodbye to a twenty-six-year marriage I thought would last forever, my journey has taken more unexpected twists and turns than I ever could have predicted. Much like the roads I've traveled.

It was the Spring of 2022, and I was fifty-two when this wild idea struck me: to go to each of the fifty states, searching for something deeper than the usual tourist spots. But how could I make it meaningful? Then it hit me: The true magic of a place isn't just in its landmarks, but in the people you meet. What if, despite all our perceived differences and the political and social divides permeating our country, I could find connection simply by breaking bread with a stranger? I wondered if I, in my own small way, could help fuel connections and community across our beloved country. And that's how my 50 States Project was born.

Through most of my fifty-third year, in 2023, I turned this dream into reality. By the time my fifty-fourth birthday rolled around in December, I found myself filing for divorce. Now, finishing up this manuscript in August 2024, riding the rollercoaster of divorce, I've woven in my personal diary entries, pouring my heart and soul into these pages.

Revisiting these stories as I edit—remembering each woman and being inspired by the connection we felt as we shared pieces of our lives—has given me the confidence to move forward. I now believe that the unexpected sharp turns on the road of life, although sometimes treacherous, can be bordered by the most spectacular landscapes.

It's been one heck of a ride. With all the lessons learned and strength gained, I'm excited for whatever comes next—even if I'm not quite sure what that is yet. Thanks for taking this wild, imperfectly perfect journey with me.

With all my heart,

Shari

Dedication

The Universe has a plan.

My Japanese American parents adopted me at eleven months of age from Seoul, South Korea in 1970.

My dad was born on Main Street in Seattle in 1922. My mom was born in 1929 on Bainbridge Island, which is a short ferry ride away. On December 7, 1941, the course of their lives along with the lives of many other Americans of their generation changed forever. My dad, who was nineteen years old at the time, once told me that he will never forget the voice of the announcer on the radio who reported that Japan had bombed Pearl Harbor. My dad's heart dropped. He remembered instantly feeling anguish and disbelief. *What now is going to happen to us?* he wondered. As it turns out, just a little over two months later, President Franklin D. Roosevelt signed Executive Order 9066, which led to the forced internment of about 120,000 Japanese Americans, including my dad and his family and my mom and her family.

My dad was the oldest son of four. His family, being traditional in their Japanese way of thinking, considered the oldest son as the most important of all the children. Interestingly, my dad's father—my grandfather—was the youngest son of a very successful family in Tokyo. From all accounts, my grandfather was considered the failure of the family. After my grandfather died, we found several pencil sketches that were signed by him tucked away in his personal belongings. It is probable that his artistic nature didn't align with his parents' focus on traditional education, at which his older brothers excelled.

My grandfather arrived in the United States as a teenager, traveling alone by ship. A few years later, a marriage was arranged for him to a woman he'd never met; she was sent to the United States to meet him, traveling by ship. My grandmother had also come from a prominent Tokyo family. But upon arrival in America with no English skills, her available employment was limited. She worked for years as a motel maid. Whenever I check out of a hotel and leave a gratuity for the housecleaning staff, I think of my grandmother—a woman who passed away before I was born and who my dad always spoke of fondly. I always include a handwritten note of thanks, in her honor.

My dad was raised with the mandate from his parents that he must do no wrong because it would be an embarrassment not only to his family but also to the Japanese community. The Japanese immigrant community wanted to prove themselves as trustworthy and loyal Americans. He was also raised by his parents to believe that he had to perform three times better than his White counterparts in order to receive equal treatment. When my dad reached adulthood, he was very critical of the pressures his parents had placed on him, which led him to be risk averse. As a result, he held himself back from taking on challenges that carried a possibility of failure.

My mom's childhood was very different from my dad's. She was the ninth child of ten. She had eight older brothers and one younger sister. Being younger, she didn't face the pressures my dad had had to deal with. She processed her internment camp experience very differently from the way he did. For her, being in an internment camp was a chance for her "to live with her friends." Being a middle-schooler at the time, her focus was very much in the moment, centered around her circle of friends, rather than on the emotional turmoil and mental anguish my dad experienced as a young man. When the internment order of anyone with Japanese blood was issued, it included even those with just 1/16th of Japanese ancestry.

Before World War II ended, five of my mother's brothers had served in an all-Japanese unit of the Army, the highly honored and most decorated United States Army unit of World War II: the 442nd Infantry. At one time,

DEDICATION

my grandmother had five yellow hearts in her internment camp barrack window, representing all her sons who were fighting for the United States.

I'm certain my mom would have loved to travel, but my dad didn't feel that travel would be comfortable or safe for a family that looked like ours—Asian Americans. He didn't feel that we would be accepted in all parts of the country because of his experience as a Japanese American during WWII and the experiences that followed throughout his life. As such, my travel experiences as a child were limited to the Western states.

Unwittingly, I took on my dad's belief: that I wasn't welcome everywhere based on my Asian features.

In part, I embarked on the 50 States Project to rewrite these limiting beliefs, which had shaped my childhood. Instead of supposing that I would not be welcome or accepted, I chose to step out with the belief that *I'm welcome everywhere*. And it was with this energy and openness that I traveled to places I never dreamed I would travel to as a child.

This decision to travel through the United States to meet with fifty strangers very quickly had a profound effect on the way I see the world. Even the simple act of connecting with women to ask if they would be a part of my project surprised me. The willingness of strangers to take time out of their busy lives to meet with me to share a meal has taught me that miracles can happen when you make the first move. I've found that most of us want to feel connected to one another—and because of this, we are more open than perhaps we realize to explore new connections despite any preconceived differences. If given the right nudge.

What also surprised me was that the only recurring theme of slight reluctance I encountered when seeking women to connect with was, "I don't know if I'm interesting enough for you." My hope is that my journey will help everyone who reads this book to realize how worthy and interesting every person is—and that even the briefest of meetings can change someone's life. These fifty women have changed my life for the better. Each one has a special place in my heart.

I wish my dad were alive now to witness me challenging his beliefs, and that he could find out what I discovered: *I am welcome everywhere, and everything is available to me.*

I am certain that my dad would understand and support my journey of self-discovery. I know he would have been my biggest cheerleader as he watched me open a new chapter—taking on the starring role in my own life.

Dad, this project is dedicated to you. I miss you.

RIP Henry Aoyama
September 19, 1922–January 25, 2001

Table for Two

Whenever things begin to feel like too much, I've learned that the best thing I can do is to take a deep breath, and start with something small. At first, trying to meet fifty women from fifty different states felt like a huge, almost impossible project. But I decided to tackle it one tiny step at a time. Kind of like how you eat an elephant—one bite at a time; right?

I started by reconnecting with women I'd interacted with through my work over the past three years, including podcasters and vendors. These were women I had emailed or chatted with but had never met in person. I also reached out to women from my past—some I had only met briefly and others whom I had lost touch with over the last three decades or so. It felt like opening a time capsule. From these efforts, I connected with twenty-seven incredible women across twenty-seven states who were willing to meet up with me.

Next, I posted about my project in an online professional group that I was a member of, listing the states where I still needed to find connections. To my surprise, responses flooded in from women eager to help me reach my goal, referring me to people they knew in those states. Social media also contributed, with more friends and connections offering assistance. Finally, with thirteen states still left and no referrals from colleagues or online friends, I turned to the internet. I searched for women who were business owners in the remaining states, figuring that their established roots there would lessen the chances of me being stood up.

By April 6, 2022, I had managed to line up meetings with women from all fifty states. It had been less than a month, and I had already laid down a network of connections across the entire country.

While I was hopeful all the women would follow through, I knew anything could happen over the course of a year. To manage this, I planned my follow-ups carefully. I hired Carissa, who proved to be a reliable Virtual Assistant based out of the Philippines; she helped me implement a check-in plan. We touched base regularly with each woman: six months, three months, one month, two weeks, and one week before each planned visit. One of my biggest worries was flying all that way only to find out they wouldn't show. The travel kept me busy, sometimes traveling to multiple states in a day. Also affecting my itinerary were the media interviews along the way, which kept my calendar full and gave me reason to stay in some states to visit for a day or two longer than initially planned.

With a little encouragement from friends, support from my family, and the courage of these women to meet someone they had never known, I discovered something important: Deep down, we all seek connection with one another.

Because when you get right down to it, we're not built to walk through this world all on our own.

"Table for two, please."

July 21, **2022**

Dear Diary,

Today was a big day: my biannual check-up at Fred Hutch Cancer Center. It's hard to believe it's been nearly five years since I first walked through those doors, diagnosed with breast cancer. Every time I sit in that waiting room, a whirlwind of emotions hits me. This morning, I peeked at my lab results through the electronic chart before meeting with my oncologist. Just like it's been for the past eight years, my white blood cell count and neutrophil count are still below the normal range. I really wish my doctors could figure out why, but for now, all they can say is that my "normal" might just be a bit lower than what's typical. Fingers crossed that's all it is.

In six months, I'll hit the five-year mark of having No Evidence of Disease! Just thinking about that possibility makes me tear up.

Driving home after today's appointment, I couldn't stop thinking about my 50 States Project and all the incredible people I'm going to meet as I travel across the country. This morning's visit reminded me how important it is to make the most out of every single day. I'm all-in—not just on traveling, but also on meeting and learning from as many people as I can while I have the chance.

Feeling all the feels,

Shari

January 7, **2023**

Dear Diary,

I'm smiling at a few little lucky moments. I received a free upgrade—from coach to first class—from Alaska Airlines. And Hilton upgraded my room without me even requesting it, and I arrived at the hotel at 7:10 PM and was given room 710. It all feels magical!

On a side note, I found out that Netflix is based in Albuquerque. I had no idea. Netflix is here! OK, I'm just going to put it out there into the universe: *Netflix, do you hear me? I'm just down the street. Interested in promoting friendships and unity with me as I travel across the United States of America?*

Let the adventure begin,

Shari

TRAVEL LOG

January 7, 2023

Nicole and me at Sawmill Market, Albuquerque, New Mexico

Table 1

Coffee at Sawmill Market
Albuquerque, New Mexico

Nicole
Sunday, January 8, 2023—9:00 AM MST

Nicole is thirty-four years old. She was born and raised in New Mexico, she's married to her husband of ten years, and she is mother to two young sons. A former K–12 teacher, she now owns her own business, Nicole Bridges Photography, LLC.

I was practically bubbling with excitement as I prepared for the launch of my project. I was all set to meet with a woman from New Mexico, someone a friend had recommended. But then, just a few weeks before my flight to Albuquerque, she vanished. No responses to my emails, no confirmations of our meeting time and place. It was like she had disappeared into thin air, and I couldn't help but wonder if this was a bad omen for my entire project.

With a mix of hope and anxiety, I threw myself back into the search for someone to meet. Without any connections in New Mexico, I resorted to cold calling after a thorough internet search. I decided to look for women who owned businesses in New Mexico, reasoning that they would be more likely to stick to a schedule. After sifting through profiles of everyone from lawyers to life coaches, I stumbled upon Nicole's Instagram account. Her feed, filled with regular updates of her photography work, reassured me that she was as dedicated to her commitments as she was to her craft.

Reaching out to Nicole felt like a big risk, but the moment she agreed to meet, I felt an enormous sense of relief. Nicole's consistent communication was an initial victory. It taught me that sometimes, you just have to take a leap of faith and hope for the best if you want to see the magic happen.

Our meeting unfolded under the expansive blue skies of a chilly New Mexico morning. Nicole chose Old Town Plaza for our rendezvous—the vibrant heart of the city, which captures the rich history and spirit of Albuquerque. Up until then, we'd only connected through texts, but I had a plan to ensure she'd show up: I'd booked a quick photo session with her. Part of me wanted to capture our meeting forever in a photo; the other part thought offering a paid gig would ensure she showed up. Looking back, I realize my little scheme was unnecessary. Nicole is as genuine as they come—a person you meet once and trust instantly.

From the moment we greeted each other with a hug, it felt like rediscovering a long-lost friend. We exchanged gifts—I gave her my latest book, *Ask Yourself This*, and she gave me a curated bag of goodies from Albuquerque—and there wasn't a trace of awkwardness. Just genuine enthusiasm mixed with a bit of nervous excitement. We began with our mini photo session, strolling through the streets of Old Town Albuquerque, soaking in the sights and the rich Mexican culture that permeates the city. Afterward, we headed to a popular food court marketplace, Sawmill Market, which reminded me of a smaller version of New York City's Chelsea Market, with its variety of small specialty restaurants and palpable vibrant energy.

Over shared morning coffee and a snack, Nicole opened up about her family—her husband, and how they met, and their two young sons. She also talked about the challenges they faced when her father was diagnosed with Huntington's Disease in 2017 (the same year I was battling breast cancer).

TABLE 1

While I recognized the name of the disease, I wasn't sure exactly what it entailed. Nicole explained that Huntington's Disease is a tough, inherited condition that affects the brain. It gradually causes the brain cells to break down, leading to problems with movement, thinking, and emotions. She described it as a mix of Alzheimer's, Parkinson's, and ALS all rolled into one. Symptoms usually start in a person's thirties or forties, but they can appear earlier or later. Over time, the disease worsens, making everyday activities increasingly difficult. It's genetic, meaning that if a parent has it, there's a fifty-percent chance their child will too. This makes it challenging not only for the person with the disease but also for their family.

Her father's diagnosis changed Nicole's life forever. Her father, like me, was adopted, and he found his birth family just before his shocking diagnosis, which sped up the identification of the disease that had affected other members of his birth family. With a fifty-percent chance of carrying the genetic marker, Nicole worried about her own health and that of her sons. After struggling to process her father's news, she made a decision. Instead of getting tested—since a positive result wouldn't change anything—Nicole chose to live her life as if she had the diagnosis. She decided to live as healthily and fully as possible, not wasting a single day.

I told her that I had made the same decision back in 2017 after my cancer diagnosis. Sitting across from each other at the breakfast table, we realized we had both experienced the same pivotal year, which led us each to resolve to embrace life, to cherish every moment, and to live to the fullest. I explained to her that, in part, the 50 States Project is a testament to my determination to live this way.

In those precious hours, Nicole and I saw reflections of ourselves in each other's stories—how 2017 reshaped and strengthened us, despite the dark moments. Our goodbye was filled with glints of tears in our eyes, not from sorrow but from the joy of finding a soul sister. Both of us understood that stepping out to share a meal with a stranger was exactly in line with our commitment to embrace opportunities and cherish every day.

I couldn't have dreamed of a better start than meeting someone who, unbeknownst to me until that morning, had chosen to embrace each day—in the exact same year I had decided to do the same.

The thrill of what lay ahead with the next forty-nine stops had me buzzing. I was ready for each story, each connection—willing to pour my whole heart into every conversation and wondering if they would all flow as seamlessly as this one did.

January 12, **2023**

Dear Diary,

Guess what? I'm writing to you from the sun-kissed beaches of Hawaii—a place so breathtaking, I keep pinching myself to make sure I'm not dreaming! It's funny, I always say Hawaii feels like a sneak-peek of heaven: a place where the faces look a lot like mine and English fills the air. As an Asian American, it's the only place on Earth where I look and sound like the majority.

Every time I'm here, I can't help but think of Dad. He used to say that Hawaii was the only place where he ever felt like he truly fit in—where he didn't feel different. He saw his reflection in the people around him, and they understood each other perfectly. It's kind of emotional to think about him finding a slice of belonging, even if it was just for a little while. Being here, sitting outside, in front of my hotel, taking in the sights and sounds around me, I'm absorbing what he felt.

But oh, Diary, I've got some thrilling news to spill! Just as I was soaking up the island vibes, a text from Kourtney Jason, the world's best publicist, who's been my right hand for three years, messaged me. Could it be? That *The Today Show* has actually invited me to bring my story to living rooms across the country?

Yup, it's happening! *The Today Show* wants me to come on and share all about my adventures and about the amazing souls I'm sharing meals with throughout my travels for this project. I'm over the moon! This is one of those moments where everything feels monumental.

I can't stop smiling—and I don't want to stop.

Feeling the aloha spirit through and through,

Shari

TRAVEL LOG

January 12, 2023

Nancy and me at Prince Waikiki Hotel, Honolulu, Hawaii

Table 2

Poolside Drinks and Bites at Prince Waikiki Hotel
Honolulu, Oahu, Hawaii

Nancy
Saturday, January 14, 2023—11:00 AM Hawaii–Aleutian Time

Nancy is thirty-eight years old, and she has resided in Hawaii since she was eight years of age, growing up in Oahu. She currently lives on the Island of Hawaii with her husband and their young daughter. She works as an Executive Director of a non-profit serving children and families.

I couldn't believe Nancy was flying from the Island of Hawaii to Oahu to share a meal with me. Her efforts to make travel easier for me, knowing it was less expensive for me to fly from Seattle to Oahu than to the Island of Hawaii felt like a generous gift.

When it comes to appointments and meetings, I'm usually on time—almost religiously so—but fate had other plans. Instead of arriving at the Prince Waikiki Hotel, I somehow ended up at the Royal Hawaiian Resort. I know, right? After wandering around in circles, trying to find the poolside bar where Nancy and I were supposed to meet, I finally asked an employee for help. That's when I realized my mistake.

Nancy just laughed when I called to explain. She remarked, "You're not late, you're on Hawaiian time." Just like that, all my worries about being late melted away. She made me feel like I belonged.

Our encounter started with Nancy draping a beautiful lei around my neck—a gesture steeped in a Hawaiian tradition of love. It felt like the perfect embrace to welcome me into the next leg of my 50 States Project.

It is hard to believe that just a week earlier, I was soaking up the scene in Albuquerque, New Mexico. There, I had met Nicole, and just before flying home to Seattle, I dropped by a local wine-tasting room. I ended up chatting with Daniel, a young man raised in what locals call Albuquerque's "War Zone." He shared stories of his life, brimming with rich Mexican family traditions.

Interestingly, I learned that Nancy's heritage was similar to Daniel's: Her parents hailed from Mexico too. Listening to her recount tales of her upbringing, laced with the same cultural richness and distinct expectations for sons and daughters, I felt a seamless connection between my conversation with Daniel and my time with Nancy—a natural segue divinely designed.

With Nancy, what was scheduled as a two-hour chat unfurled into four. We traded life stories as we sipped on delicious Hawaiian-themed cocktails and poolside appetizers. Nancy's account of her daughter's premature birth at just twenty-six weeks really drew me in. Her daughter was a tiny fighter from the very beginning. As Nancy shared the harrowing story—of not only almost losing her daughter, but also of nearly losing her own life during the birth and the weeks that followed—I couldn't help but glance over to the pool, which was several feet away where Nancy's husband and daughter (now a healthy toddler) were laughing and playing.

Listening to Nancy describe her daughter's birth during the height of the pandemic felt like stepping into a world filled with true *aloha* spirit. She shared how she and her husband received so much help—not just from friends and family but also from strangers, including those in their Bahá'í faith community. People offered them a place to stay, a car, and help with bills. It was a wonderful illustration of aloha as well as *ohana*—where family ties extend beyond bloodlines for love and support.

As an adoptee who was orphaned and unable to find my birth family, I am particularly drawn to the belief that family connections can be found anywhere. Like my dad said, there's something profoundly comforting about finding a place where you truly belong. And I deeply felt that belonging—that aloha and ohana spirit—during my time with Nancy.

January 15, **2023**

Dear Diary,

You won't believe what's been going on. So, my husband decided to join me on this trip to Hawaii. It is one of five states where he has chosen to join me on my travels. And honestly, just between us, it's been stirring up so much angst inside me. It seems like no matter where we go together, there's always that inevitable day when his drinking leads to a fight. It is a pattern that has been happening for years. Hawaii, with all its splendor, couldn't escape our pattern.

When he is sober, he is smart, kind, and handsome—the whole package. But when he drinks, it's like he becomes someone else, someone I can't connect with, someone I don't recognize. He'd probably say he's just unwinding, like anyone would on vacation. And I get that. I've had my moments, too. But it's different with him. The personality change and excess drinking hurts me to my core.

I'm trying desperately to hold onto that aloha spirit that I felt yesterday with Nancy, but it's tough. I dream of a trip where this tension isn't looming over us. Is this normal for couples? We've been together since we were twenty-five years old, and it's like we don't know any other way to be.

I don't believe he truly understands the depth of my pain, and perhaps I'm also not fully recognizing his.

Wishing for peace in paradise,

Shari

TRAVEL LOG

January 18, 2023

Anna and me at her home, Paradise Valley, Arizona

Table 3

Lunch at Anna's Home
Paradise Valley, Arizona

Anna
Friday, January 20, 2023—11:00 AM MST

Anna is fifty-three years old and a single mom to two young adults—a son and a daughter. She was born in Los Angeles, has lived in other states, and for the past several years she has made Arizona her home. She is an artist, art curator, and owner of a small art gallery.

Landing in Arizona always brings a wave of calm over me, like I'm enveloping myself in those vast, serene desert vibes that I've come to love. This time was extra special because I got to stay at the glitzy Biltmore Resort for free, thanks to a stash of hotel points. The Biltmore isn't just a hotel to me; it's a treasure trove of family memories—a place that, despite its facelifts over the years, still whispers stories of old Hollywood glam and Frank Lloyd Wright's architectural magic.

But on this trip, it wasn't just about reliving those family getaways. I was stepping into a whole new world: television! My first ever in-studio TV interview was on the horizon, and the thrill was real. I had landed a spot on *Arizona Daily Mix*, right after the hosts discussed Tom Hanks' latest quirky beverage concoction, "Diet Cokagne"—a blend of Diet Coke and

Champagne. I made a mental note to give that mix a try; it sounded like the perfect icebreaker for my next gathering back home.

The excitement spilled over into the next day with a bright and early feature on *Good Morning Arizona*. There I was, live on TV, feeling like I needed someone to pinch me to confirm this wasn't all just a vivid dream.

Amid the whirlwind of media appearances, a truly heartfelt experience awaited me at Anna's home. She had a beautiful luncheon with a gathering of her female friends planned for that afternoon, and I was invited. Walking into her space felt like stepping into a world where every corner, every piece, had a story, and a purpose. Her home was a living mosaic of unique vintage items, thrift store finds, and striking art pieces—all reflecting the wonderful complexity of Anna's life and connections. Her doormat, cheerfully proclaiming YAY, YOU'RE HERE couldn't have captured her essence any better.

Having lunch at Anna's, I felt like I was living inside one of those adventure novels, where every character is vibrant and bursting with stories. Each woman at the table, coming from a different walk of life, had her own tale to tell.

Among them was Betty, who at ninety-three was nothing short of a whirlwind. She showed me the endless charm of making new friends, no matter your age, and the importance of keeping those connections alive through the years. Betty was a living example of the fact that getting older doesn't mean shutting out new experiences. Instead, aging is an opportunity to open new doors to new relationships.

While I learned that Anna and I have walked different paths, we met at the same crossroads: We see life as one big classroom, and each person we meet opens a new chapter of lessons. Her home, filled with laughter and stories, reflected the balance and purpose she carries within her. It was a powerful lesson on living a life that rings true to who you really are.

Back home in Seattle, my own place felt a bit off, as if it were just a meticulously set stage but without Arizona's depth of connection, which I'd

TABLE 3

felt so strongly at Anna's. It made me wonder why I felt more at home in spaces that weren't my own.

I sensed a little whisper from my soul, urging me to pay attention. I decided I want to create a new space where I can surround myself with colors, textures, and treasures that resonate with my spirit. I felt a call to align my outer world with my inner truths, just as beautifully as Anna had done.

February 2, **2024**

Dear Diary,

Here I am, in the middle of editing my manuscript, and it strikes me: It's been two and a half months since this whole divorce process began. It's strange, in a way, to find myself feeling a sense of gratitude as I look back over my emotional rollercoaster year of 2023.

My soon-to-be ex-husband and I have hired a friend, Jen Cameron, Managing Partner at The Agency Seattle, to help us sell our house. It's a big step, and I'm trying hard not to get too caught up in the house or the financial what-ifs of the divorce. It's been a real challenge, not knowing what my finances will look like. At the start, the worry was overwhelming, keeping me up at night. Fear had its grip on me—the fear of being on my own, of embracing a new identity as a divorced woman, of financial insecurity. It's funny, in a not-so-funny way, how those fears were for the most part what kept me tethered for so long to a marriage that was no longer working.

But there came a point where the fear of staying in a toxic relationship became more daunting than the fear of losing material comforts. That was a pivotal moment for me.

Rereading the section about my visit to Anna's place has been quite introspective. Her Arizona home was a sanctuary—a peaceful space that was as beautiful as she was—reflecting her personality and style. It really spoke to my soul. It's made me think about the future, about creating my own space that truly reflects who I am and what I value.

I'm inspired now to recreate that sense of peace that I felt at Anna's. It feels like an important step in this new chapter of my life.

Until next time,

Shari

January 25, **2023**

Dear Diary,

Today's one of those days that's brought a big avalanche of feelings, a day that's etched deep into my heart and soul. It's been twenty-one whole years since I had to say the hardest goodbye ever to Dad. The ache of missing him hasn't exactly disappeared; it's just gotten a bit more bearable with time. And in a twist that still feels surreal, today's also the day we celebrate Mom turning ninety-four. It's so strange and tragic that Dad's heart gave out on Mom's birthday all those years ago.

In the swirl of all these emotions, I had this super-important appointment at the Fred Hutch Cancer Center. Sitting there, waiting for my oncologist to come in, felt like forever. But then he said those magic words, "Congratulations, you've made it to five years with no evidence of disease." I realized at that moment that I had been holding my breath since my diagnosis. And I finally exhaled.

So here I am on this January 25th, tangled up in all these feelings: grief for my dad, thoughts about my mom, and a heart full of thanks for health—along with excitement for what's ahead.

Dad, if you're somewhere out there listening, I want you to know that I feel like you're right here with me, celebrating my good health, and maybe giving me one of your reassuring pats on the back, whispering, "Keep going." Your spirit, your wisdom, it's all still with me, lighting my way. As I hold you close in my heart, it feels like we're on this adventure together, exploring the United States for the very first time.

Feeling overwhelmed and grateful—and thankfully, in good health,

Shari

TRAVEL LOG

January 27, 2023

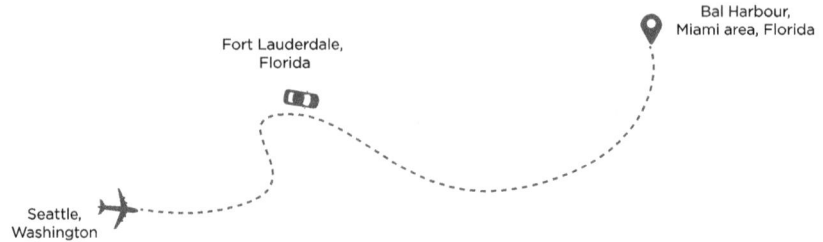

Paula and me at Le Zoo, Bal Harbour, Florida

Table 4

Lunch at Le Zoo
Bal Harbour, Florida

Paula
Sunday, January 29, 2023—12:00 Noon EST

Paula is a forty-two-year-old married woman. Her mother was born in Puerto Rico and is of Spanish and Portuguese descent, while her father is from Brooklyn, New York of Italian descent. She was born in New York and moved to Florida during the pandemic.

The day I finally got to meet Paula face to face felt like opening a door to a room filled with sunlight. She is an author and national speaker. Thinking back to the year 2020—when my debut book, *The 50/50 Friendship Flow: Life Lessons From And For My Girlfriends*, was launched into the big, wide world—Paula was my North Star in the whole crazy media galaxy of on-camera interviews. Her smart advice—especially about always saying thank-you to the folks behind the scenes after going on TV—helped me build real, lasting friendships and connections. She always says that a simple expression of gratitude will take you miles. Paula made a huge difference in my career, as my first book soon developed into a three-volume series.

I totally get Paula. I feel like if we were in high school together, we would have been natural friends. In addition to being a media coach, she is also a list-making professional, teaching others through her talks and books how to make life more manageable through list-making. A habitual list-maker myself, I love the way she seamlessly manages her busy life. Our mutual love of lists is more than just about keeping things in order; it's like choreographing calm in the middle of a storm. My 50 States Project is blossoming from that same love for planning things out.

But it's more than just lists and work stuff between us. At this lunch, shared at a trendy Miami Beach French bistro, with oysters and bubbles—*hello, perfection!*—Paula opened up about her quest for dual citizenship in Italy, and her roots search in Spain and Portugal. It was like holding up a mirror to my own quiet thoughts about South Korea, the place where I was born but haven't really explored. It has been like a distant dream, waiting for the "right" moment, and I'm sort of scared that I won't fit in. I think I'm afraid of feeling like a foreigner in my own birth country—that even the country I was born in won't feel like home.

As I listened to Paula, a door in my mind creaked open, shedding light on a possibility I'd never even dusted off for consideration: dual citizenship with South Korea. It's funny how a simple conversation over lunch can turn your perspective inside out. Paula showed me that it's not about picking sides, like choosing teams in gym class. It's about embracing the whole of who you are. Our talk sparked a yearning in me—a real curiosity about what it would be like to wander the streets of my birthplace once this project wraps up.

So there I was, driving to the airport, lost in thought about what *home* really means. It had become something much deeper than just finding the perfect address. It was turning into a question that reached into my soul, asking not just where I fit in, but how many places could hold a piece of my heart. *Maybe it's not about choosing one location over another*, I thought, *but about embracing the richness of life's "ands."* Maybe home isn't a single spot on a map. Maybe

TABLE 4

home is found in lots of different surroundings, moments, and memories. Right at that moment, feeling a bit disconnected from my own space that I called home, I could only wonder.

Me with my adoptive parents, circa 1975

February 5, **2023**

Dear Diary,

This weekend, I was in Los Angeles for the MusiCares Person of the Year Award, soaking in the city's sparkle and energy. Little did I know it would be the backdrop for the third most painful phone call of my life. The first was when I learned of Dad's death in 2001. The second was in 2017, when my doctor told me my breast biopsy was positive for cancer. And then, just two days ago, while I was in my hotel room, I saw the caller ID from Mom's retirement community. With a knot in my stomach, I answered. A voice I didn't recognize told me that Mom, Lillian, had been found dead in her apartment. She was gone.

You might expect me to fill these pages with tender memories and raw grief. But the story of Mom and me isn't like that. It's complicated, filled with a quiet heartbreak. To the outside world, she was kindness and love personified—the woman who, along with her husband, adopted an orphan from South Korea. But to me, she was the source of my perpetual longing. I always felt like an outsider, a shadow in her busy world.

Maybe it was the complexities of my adoption—the journey through multiple caretakers before landing in her home—that strained our bond. Or perhaps it was her pain, seeing the easy affection between her nieces and nephews and their parents, a stark contrast to our interactions, which left us both trapped in a cycle of mutual disappointment.

Now, with her passing, relatives who haven't reached out in over a decade are suddenly reappearing, offering condolences that feel hollow, considering their absence during the isolating months of the COVID-19 pandemic when I was the only one attending to her needs. The hypocrisy stings.

What haunts me the most is the silent tragedy of her life: She was a mother who passed away without ever experiencing the kind of warmth and connection I cherish with my own children. I hope that somehow, in the afterlife, we can find a way to bridge the chasm that always stretched between us in life.

Rest in peace, Mom. It breaks my heart that, while I've managed to create meaningful relationships with strangers, you and I could never forge the bond we both so desperately sought.

With a heavy heart,

Shari

February 3, **2024**

Dear Diary,

Last night was one of those moments when frustration got the better of me, especially dealing with The Past (Yep, that's what I've dubbed my almost-ex-husband in my phone. So, when he texts or calls, my phone alerts me that The Past is calling—which gives me a smile). Halfway through my rant, I had a moment of clarity: All this anger was just a waste of energy, only succeeding in sending my stress levels skyrocketing. Utterly pointless.

It dawned on me, especially poignant as we mark a year since Mom passed away, that my marriage mirrored my relationship with her in many ways. Both were fundamental mismatches. Mom was always lost in her religious fervor, and my soon-to-be-ex-husband was ensnared by his love affair with alcohol.

I poured my heart and soul into both relationships—I really did—only to realize I was beginning to lose myself in the process. Sadly, with both of them, my attempts and my words simply evaporated. It's clear now: I was never the protagonist in their narratives.

But there's a shift happening now. I'm finally stepping into the spotlight of my own story. I'm learning to release the anger and the emotions that prevent me from savoring the beauty of the present.

And the quest for my true leading man? It's officially begun.

Sending out all my love,

Shari

February 23, **2023**

Hey Diary,

What a whirlwind this month has been! Right after getting back from L.A., I found myself sifting through my mom's apartment, boxing up memories. It's strange, touching her things—her books (all written by those staunchly conservative Christian authors), her signed Melania Trump posters, and those Trump coins. It's like each item is a loud reminder of how different our beliefs were, and how we each gravitated toward very different types of people. But it's not just her political or religious beliefs that caught my eye. Many of my friends are devout Christians or staunch Republicans. It's the sheer *volume* of her memorabilia, books, and donation receipts that really underscores her extremism—especially when I think about my own moderate leanings.

Then, *bam*, my husband and I were off to Egypt! Honestly, I was nervous. We've been a bit off, and on top of that, I'm freaking out about a dance competition for a Seattle charity that's coming up soon. (Hold on, I'll spill the tea on the dance thing in a bit!) But guess what? Egypt turned out to be the break I didn't know I needed. Ten days spent in Egypt felt like magic.

Now, I'm chilling in Cairo at our hotel, about to head back to the USA, and the vibe here is giving me some big-city energy, kind of like L.A. or New York. The view from our hotel is just wow! It screams ancient but also new. And Nemo—our Egyptologist—she's a riot. She made the whole trip unforgettable.

My biggest takeaway: the people. Everyone's been so kind and welcoming. The kids, the shopkeepers, our guides, and even how they care for stray animals adds to the warmth of this region. Karim—our local guide—with his laughter and stories, has made me see things differently. Instead of viewing the Middle East with fear—a perspective shaped by the frightening images in the media—I experienced love and a warm, welcoming spirit.

Karim's description of the misconceptions about his country hit home, making me think about how the stories we tell shape us, and the importance of seeking truth. It's a lesson I'm taking with me back to the States. The locals here made me blush with their compliments—telling my husband that he hit the jackpot because I look like Queen Nefertari. It's those fun moments of laughing with strangers that remind me that we're all in this together, no matter where we are in the world.

And you know what? I felt safe here, more than I sometimes do in big cities back home. It's probably naïve, but it's true.

Leaving Egypt, Karim's words about sharing the real story of this place have stuck with me. The stories of the hard-working shopkeepers, the joy I witnessed of friends greeting each other on the streets, and the love and closeness demonstrated amongst family members—it fills my heart. Returning to the States with these memories and stories to share reminds me of what I hope my 50 States Project grows into: an adventure that reveals the beauty in our country and its people.

With wanderlust,

Shari

Old Cairo, Egypt, February 2023

I met this beautiful woman—and I wish I had written down her name. While I unfortunately do not remember her name, I remember its meaning. She told me that her name in Arabic means Sunshine. *She is my age, and she says she has been selling lemons all of her life.*

TRAVEL LOG

March 1, 2023

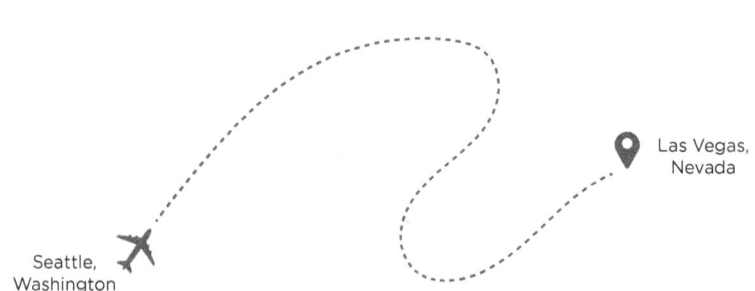

Catherine and me at Mon Ami Gabi, Las Vegas, Nevada

Table 5

Lunch at Mon Ami Gabi
Las Vegas, Nevada

Catherine
Thursday, March 2, 2023—1:00 PM PST

Catherine is fifty-seven years old. She was widowed at a young age after approximately nine years of marriage—losing her husband, who was a professional baseball player, to cancer. She never remarried but after many years she's currently engaged. She was raised in Lewiston, Idaho and now calls Las Vegas her home.

For the longest time, Catherine and I were just faces behind screens. As we had originally connected on social media because of our many mutual friends, our friendship was an array of "likes" and heart emojis, as we shared snippets of our lives through Facebook updates. Her posts, always so vivid and joyful, left me curious about the stories they concealed. So, when I planned a trip to Nevada, Catherine instantly sprang to mind.

I'd only been to Las Vegas a handful of times, my experience with its dazzling neon landscape somewhat superficial. I asked Catherine to choose where we'd meet, and she picked Mon Ami Gabi at the Hotel Paris, a spot with breathtaking views of the Las Vegas Strip—the iconic Bellagio Fountain across the street. This was my first visit to this restaurant, and upon arriving, I knew instantly it was a place I'd be drawn back to—a new favorite.

Stepping onto the bustling patio, I wondered if I'd recognize Catherine from her pictures alone. Our friendship, after all, had unfolded in pixels and posts. As it turned out, we recognized one another immediately. It was as if we'd known each other in a life beyond digital—with a tangible kinship. We were dressed almost identically—both wearing black pants, black shirts, and tan jackets—which made us laugh. Beneath that laughter was the recognition of something deeper, an unspoken connection.

As we chatted, Catherine's life pieced together like a jigsaw puzzle. She knew plenty about me from my candid social media presence, while she tended to keep her deeper stories just beyond the public eye. Today, I had the privilege of hearing her stories firsthand—to meet the woman behind the vibrant photos.

As we each enjoyed fabulous entrée-sized salads and sparkling wine, I was surprised to learn that her Facebook *About Me* description—*professional poker player*—wasn't just a fun nod to Vegas. It's her actual life. I was sharing a meal with a professional poker player, in Las Vegas, no less! It made me reflect on my own snap judgments, the ones we make when we don't really know someone. It took me back to times when *I* was misunderstood, simply based on my appearance.

Catherine's narrative was compelling, like something out of a novel. She had transitioned from college to entrepreneurship, and eventually to the poker tables of Las Vegas—each chapter of her life filled with unexpected twists. Her professional poker career started accidentally—with a card game at a bowling alley, where she discovered not just a knack for poker but a passion for the game. This revelation led her to bigger challenges, eventually earning her recognition—in America and abroad.

Walking away from our conversation, I felt my perspective had widened. Catherine, with her straightforward and genuine demeanor, prompted me to examine assumptions I didn't even know I held. Ready to meet forty-five more women, who would surely come from diverse backgrounds, I took a deep breath, inspired to delve deeper into my own preconceptions.

This journey, just five states in, was already reshaping my understanding of the intricate, varied tapestry of the lives that weave together to form our amazingly wonderful country. Viva Las Vegas!

March 2, **2023**

Dear Diary,

It's Zach's birthday. I love him so much! He's twenty-one today!

I remember when he was in the fourth grade, and looking directly at him, I was taken aback by his height. I remarked, "I can't believe you're so tall." He wittily replied, "Well then, I think you need glasses since I'm right here in front of you."

With that memory echoing, I'll refrain from saying "I can't believe he's twenty-one now." I wish I was able to celebrate with him today, but he lives in Los Angeles, pursuing his passions in his third year at Occidental College. He's delving deep into Cognitive Science with a double minor in Neuroscience and Biology. And while his academic success is impressive, it's his unwavering work ethic, humor, and the sheer kindness he exudes with everyone he meets that fills me with joy.

Given my own journey of adoption, Zach stands as the only soul with whom I share a bloodline. And I can see glimmers of the best of me reflected in him.

Happy Birthday, Zach!

I couldn't love him more,

Proud Mom

Happy Birthday, Zachary!

March 12, **2023**

Dear Diary,

Today, I'm resuming travel for this project, as I head to San José, California. But before I share my excitement about the trip, I must recount the unforgettable night I had.

Last evening, I took a leap of faith, stepping out of my comfort zone and dancing before a crowd to support Plymouth Housing, a Seattle non-profit organization, which holds a special place in my heart for their mission to help adults who are chronically homeless—providing them with permanent housing.

The event, *Seattle Dances*, is Seattle's version of *Dancing with the Stars*. I had the privilege of dancing with Za Thomaier, a brilliant professional dancer from Seattle. The style of dance that I was assigned was West Coast Swing. Za has not only been my dance partner but he has become a dear friend through this process.

I had been approached in the past to participate in this event. Time and time again, I declined. I was weighed down by my insecurities, worried about my double hip replacements, my problematic right ankle, my lack of a dance background, and the fear of embarrassment. The idea of asking for donations made me cringe (for this competition, money donations equal votes). In addition to dancing, each dancer must agree to bring in an expected dollar amount as part of their contribution to the event, and my own self-doubt cast shadows on my capabilities.

Yet, to my astonishment and pride, by the end of the night, Za and I held a trophy, recognized for the highest number of unique voters. Together, we managed to raise over $95K! It was a big life lesson that showed me that self-imposed fears and limiting beliefs are often the only thing holding me back—and they can even affect the impact I want to make in this world.

As I prepared for today's flight to San José, I hoped for an early night. However, with the shift from standard to daylight savings time, which I didn't realize given all the excitement until right before I went to bed, my hoped-for 2:00 AM bedtime became 3:00 AM.

Thankfully, the lack of sleep is barely a blip on my radar, as the thrill of meeting Hannah in California keeps my spirits high.

Feeling on top of the world and ready for the day's adventure—and grateful for experiencing the magic that can happen when I let go of my own self-limiting beliefs.

When you get the chance, dance,

Shari

Za and me, March 11, 2023

TRAVEL LOG

March 12, 2023

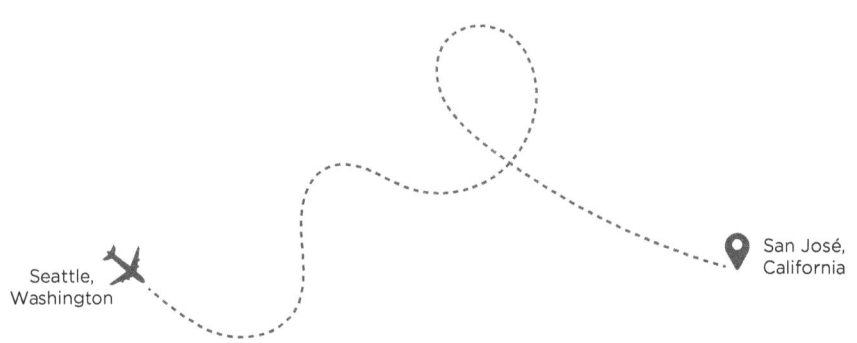

Hannah and me at La Terraza Grill & Bar, San José, California

Table 6

Lunch at La Terraza Grill & Bar
San José, California

Hannah
Monday, March 13, 2023—10:00 AM PST

Hannah is thirty-seven years old, and married with two young children—a daughter and a son. She was raised in Southington, Connecticut, and relocated to San José, California from New York in early 2020. Hannah is a classically trained vocalist who is both a performer and business owner. She owns a music academy whose primary clients are school-aged children.

When I stumbled upon Hannah, it felt like finding the missing piece in a puzzle. It was right after my first book hit the shelves in 2021, and I was on a quest for the perfect voice to breathe life into its pages. Out of all the audio-book auditions, Hannah's voice cut through the noise. It was clear, full of warmth, and it just felt right. Her professionalism made our collaboration seamless, and before we knew it, she had become the voice of the entire *Friendship Series*.

Hannah moved to California with her family just before March 2020. She and her husband are both professional singers, and they'd made the move because they both received incredible career opportunities—which were unfortunately closed down shortly after their arrival due to the pandemic.

With all professional public live music performances cancelled, Hannah's resilience came through. She turned a closed door into an open window by starting her own music academy.

In a gesture that felt like the universe nodding in approval, she offered me my first voice lesson—a thought that filled me with both excitement and a bit of dread. I mean, I've never sung in public. I've only lip-synced, faking my way even through my children's birthday parties as they were growing up. Singing out loud in front of anyone has been one of my biggest fears.

Entering the Almaden Academy of Music, I was greeted by Hannah's infectious smile, which eased my nerves instantly. The place was a haven for music lovers. Hannah, despite having opened it only six months ago, was already making positive waves in the community. It was clear she wasn't just teaching music; she was shaping futures.

My goal might have seemed small: to finally sing *Happy Birthday* out loud. But to Hannah, it was a challenge she was eager to accept. And guess what? I did sing. It was more about the heart than hitting the perfect notes—but it still felt like a win.

Following my successful voice lesson, we walked over to a nearby family-owned Colombian restaurant, La Terraza, which sits in the same strip mall as Hannah's school. We ordered tapas and soda. Over lunch, swapping stories and sharing laughs, Hannah and I connected on a level deeper than just our work—sharing stories about our friendships and families. We even found ourselves chatting about how we met our husbands, along with the joys and challenges of marriage and motherhood.

Observing her courage to start over by founding a music academy—and considering my own decision to travel across the USA, during this personally challenging time of my life, it was clear: It is amazing what can happen when we lean into the unknown, and decide to embrace life instead of resisting every turn.

And, most importantly, today I learned the joy of finding my voice—both literally and metaphorically—reminding me of the wisdom of accepting my own imperfections.

TRAVEL LOG

March 17, 2023

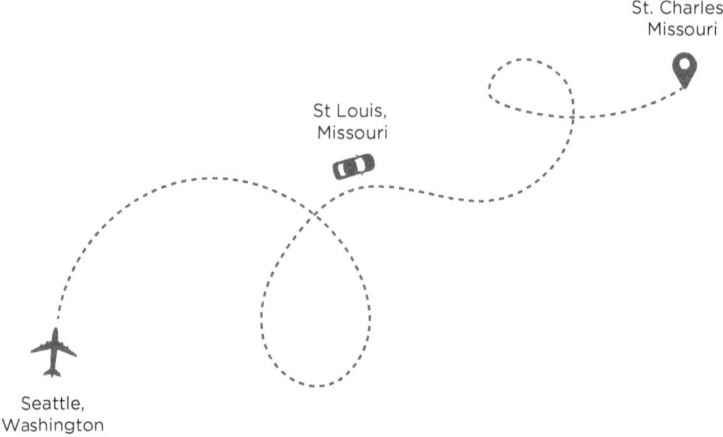

Brie and me at Prasino, St. Charles, Missouri

Table 7

Brunch at Prasino
St. Charles, Missouri

Brie
Saturday, March 18, 2023, 11:00 AM CDT

Brie is a thirty-eight-year-old woman, married to a man she started dating during her junior year of high school—a man who is two years her senior. She was born and raised in St. Charles, a place she still calls home. Brie owns a personal training studio and nutrition company.

Today felt like stepping into a scene of a favorite movie, where everyday moments shimmer with unexpected enchantment. Before meeting up with Brie in St. Charles, I found myself following my usual pre-meetup ritual: poring over the venue's online menu. My 50 States Project has had me constantly balancing the thrill of culinary discoveries with my commitment to staying healthy. It's my personal quest to ensure that this journey doesn't morph into the unexpected story of *50 States, 50 Pounds*. Imagine my surprise when I discovered that Brie had chosen a place celebrated for its organic, sustainably sourced dishes—a rare find, I imagined, in an area of the country that historically has not been known for its health-conscious eateries.

Life has a funny way of bringing together seemingly random connections. My path to meeting Brie felt like one of those beautifully orchestrated moments. During the pandemic, when everyone seemed to be binging on Netflix, my husband and I were captivated by Brie and her husband Zack's unique container home featured on the show *Amazing Interiors*. Their creative vision resonated so deeply with us that I contacted Zack, and we commissioned several pieces of his wonderful artwork. Following Brie on social media, I was drawn to her entrepreneurial spirit, along with her commitment to helping her fitness clients find their inner and outer power.

Realizing that Brie and Zack were located in Missouri, I reached out—and everything just seemed to fall into place from there. We set a date, and I felt that familiar flutter of anticipation.

Brie's warm invitation to visit their home—following our yummy lunch and lively conversation about friendship and family—was an opportunity I couldn't resist. My husband, equally intrigued by the couple whose artful living had inspired us, joined me on this journey. Their home was everything I imagined and more—every nook brimming with intention, every piece of decor telling a story of lives thoughtfully lived. The visit was more than just a visual treat; it was a journey through Brie and Zack's shared dreams and values, a glimpse into their deep respect for craftsmanship and for the environment. Meeting their rescue dog, Kokonutking, and sharing our mutual love of dogs, cemented a bond that felt like it was always meant to be.

Driven by curiosity, I asked Brie if they had ever contemplated moving to a bigger city, where Zack's art and Brie's fitness expertise might shine even brighter. Brie's response touched a chord in me. They had thought about it, but realized that the essence of home is not in the setting but in the people who fill it. For them, Missouri is more than just anyplace. It's where they grew up and where their families are. Their roots run deep.

This conversation with Brie was a gentle nudge—a reminder that spots that feel like home aren't always the ones we chase after. They're the places where we experience genuine growth and connection because of the people.

TRAVEL LOG

March 24, 2023

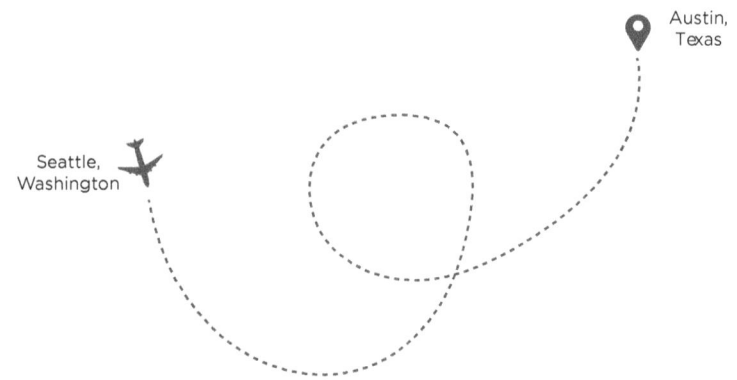

Taylor and me at Kalimotxo, Austin, TX

Table 8

Happy Hour at Kalimotxo
Austin, Texas

Taylor
Saturday, March 25, 2023—5:45 PM CDT

Taylor is twenty-nine years old, born and raised in Austin, Texas. While she has lived in other parts of the country and plans to move out of state again, she has called Austin home for the last few years. She was married at nineteen and divorced at twenty-three; she is currently single without children. She is a small business owner, working as a professional photographer.

Taylor chose the most happening spot in town for our meetup—and there couldn't have been a more perfect place to sit outside. As we sat on the patio, the sun was shining, the breeze was just right, and it seemed like everyone in sight wanted to swing by our table to say hello. Each hug and cheerful exchange with Taylor made it crystal clear: She is a magnetic soul, a real gem whose warmth and authenticity just naturally draw people to her.

Kalimotxo—named after a Spanish cocktail consisting of equal parts red wine and cola—is a vibrant Catalonian restaurant where we ordered *pintxos* (the Basque version of *tapas*). And I had my first experience of drinking from a *porrón*, which I learned is the centerpiece of the restaurant's drinks program. The glass pitcher, which can be filled with an array of Spanish wines and funky Basque ciders, is designed for patrons to imbibe straight from the spigot. Talk about setting the tone for a fun evening!

Even though there are decades between me and Taylor, when we started chatting, our age difference just melted away. It was like I was hanging out with an old friend. Maybe I was channeling my younger self, or perhaps Taylor is wise beyond her years. Probably a little of both. But one thing was absolutely certain: Taylor, still in her twenties, carries a depth and confidence that took me by surprise. As she spun a tale of her early marriage and globe-trotting adventures, her entrepreneurial spirit came through. I saw a woman who's not just finding her place in the world but boldly sculpting her life with each passing day.

Before calling it a night, we took a little tour around downtown Austin for a spontaneous photo shoot. The city bustled around us, its lively spirit the perfect backdrop. I went all-out Texas style, donning a denim skirt and top that threw back to a pop culture vibe from the early 2000s. Dressing the part has become one of the quirky joys of my travels. I like slipping into the customs of each new place I visit.

As the evening drew to a close, I realized something profound about Taylor: Observing her relentless energy and sharp intellect, I felt in my gut that I was saying goodbye to a young woman who is definitely going to leave a mark on the world through her creative photographic lens. Meeting her wasn't just fun, it was enlightening—a vital reminder of the incredible insight and untapped potential bubbling up in the younger generation. While I've always cherished the wisdom of those seasoned by life's many chapters, my time with Taylor opened my eyes to the rich perspectives of those who are just a bit younger. Taylor's distinct self-assurance, her unshakable belief in seizing life fiercely, and her quest to chase dreams without any doubt are truly inspiring.

TABLE 8

Just imagining where Taylor's exploits might take her by the time she's my age fills me with excited anticipation for what her future has in store. I can't wait to hear all the stories she'll gather along the way. And from now on, I'm making it a point to connect with her generation whenever I can. I fondly remembered my new role model, ninety-three-year-old Betty in Arizona, who keeps her life full and vibrant by continually making friends, including those of the younger generations.

TRAVEL LOG

April 1, 2023

Traci and me at Chapters Books and Coffee, Newberg, Oregon

Table 9

Newberg, Oregon
Coffee and Tea at Chapters Books and Coffee

Traci
Sunday, April 2, 2023—9:00 AM PST

Traci is fifty-two years old, born and raised in the small town of Colton, Oregon. She is married and mom to a teen-aged son. She works as a system administrator and a software developer.

Today felt like stepping into a time machine set for 1988, back when Traci and I were just a couple of eighteen-year-olds tossing our graduation caps into the air and landing at a Quaker college in Newberg, Oregon. It's funny, isn't it? How the years zip by, leaving nothing but a trail of memories. We were the late-comers that year; the college had never seen so many female co-eds before. They ran out of regular housing and ended up placing a bunch of us, including Traci and me, on a floor in what had been a guys-only dorm for over a century. Talk about making history—in a place where chapel was mandatory, and dancing was off-limits!

I was right down to the wire when I made the switch from one college to another—a decision that sounds like something straight out of one of those wild, breathless YA novels. I had everything set to start at Biola University in Los Angeles, but then, just like that, the day before I was supposed to leave, I was on the phone with the Admissions Rep at George Fox University, a Quaker college in Newberg, Oregon. I was checking to see if their acceptance offer was still on the table. Why the sudden change of heart? It was all because of a boy I'd met that Summer, who was moving to Newberg with his family. Yes, it was one of those hasty, heart-over-head decisions that only a naïve eighteen-year-old can make. And as it turns out, the relationship was over before that first full year of college came to a close.

Looking back, I can't help but marvel at how that reckless choice steered my life in such an unexpected direction. It's only now—reflecting on the timing of this project and the paths I've crossed—that I realize how deeply that decision shaped everything that followed. Meeting new people on this journey, experiencing each unexpected turn, I can't shake the feeling that there's divine intervention at play. It's as if each step, each person I meet, is carving out my life in ways I never could have imagined.

One of my clearest memories from my time at that Quaker college is taking an aerobics class that was so silent you could hear a pin drop—no music, because that would've been too close to dancing. Picture it: All of us doing the grapevine in utter silence—while somewhere, out there, Richard Simmons was probably blasting tunes and rocking out in spandex.

Our dorm floor was like a scene straight out of a teen movie, with every character archetype you could imagine. We were all hustling up and down those separate staircases for men and women, trying to figure out our place in this brave new world. Traci and I didn't stick it out for long. She found a better fit and transferred away. By my junior year, I, too, had left—transferred to the University of Washington.

Not surprisingly, life's thrown both of us some curveballs since that year we spent together in 1988. Most recently, we both faced breast cancer when our children were high school–aged. We each chose different paths to fight cancer, but we were united by the same chilling fear of not being there for our children—a fear that can still bring tears to my eyes.

Catching up today over large mugs of coffee and pastry treats, Traci confessed that she's never been one to say, "Everything happens for a reason." She pondered for a bit. Then she offered, "Maybe things happen to lead us to where we truly belong."

I've always clung to the notion that there *is* a reason behind everything, but Traci's take on it struck a deeper chord. "I am where I am meant to be."

And here I am, in the thick of my 50 States Project, feeling the weight of her words: I am exactly where the Universe wants me to be. It's a reminder I hold close, not just as I navigate the physical landscapes of the United States, but also as I chart the emotional terrain of my marriage, which seems to be on a path all its own.

TRAVEL LOG

April 2, 2023

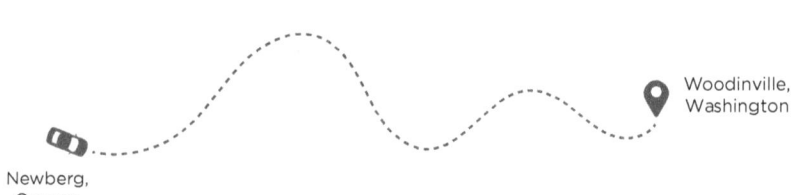

Tiernan and me at Heritage Restaurant | Bar in Woodinville, Washington

Table 10

Dinner at Heritage Restaurant | Bar
Woodinville, Washington

Tiernan
Sunday, April 2, 2023—6:00 PM PST

Tiernan is thirty-nine years old, recently married. She identifies as biracial. She—like me—is in an interracial marriage. She was born and raised in Seattle. She has no children. She works in the tech field and is also a trained theater actress and talented emcee.

Today marked a first on this whirlwind journey of mine: venturing through two states in a single day. Following my morning coffee with Traci in Newberg, Oregon, I embarked on the long drive to Woodinville, Washington. Though the trip stretched close to four hours—surprisingly more draining than any flight—the anticipation of meeting Tiernan kept my spirits high.

    I had crossed paths with Tiernan at my fundraising dance competition, just a few weeks ago. She was the emcee—a beacon of light and energy on that stage. Although we didn't get a chance to talk that day, fate seemed to wink at me when the woman I was set to meet in Washington State unexpectedly shared that she was soon moving out of state for her job. I suddenly found myself looking for someone intriguing to meet in my own home state. I immediately thought of Tiernan, there was just something about her. She'd really made an impression. So, I reached out on LinkedIn. And guess what? She was all-in for a meetup.

Over dinner, as we were just getting settled, Tiernan mentioned her upcoming fortieth birthday. I couldn't help but burst out, "The forties are where the magic happens!" I reflected on my own journey through that transformative decade—navigating health scares (which included a double hip replacement and a battle with breast cancer) and tackling parenting head-on as my children moved from grade school through middle school and on to high school. I grew in ways I'd never imagined, which included adopting a journaling practice and becoming more confident than I had ever been in earlier decades. By the time I sashayed into my fifties, I was reborn—a brand-new version of myself.

Over a shared plate of oysters and bubbles followed by delightful salads, Tiernan shared stories of her family, painting a picture so vivid I could almost see her artist parents in my mind—her father, an actor, and her mother, a classical singer. Growing up in Seattle's Scandinavian enclave with her mom, Tiernan's exploration of her identity has been nothing short of a saga. She spoke of her evolution—from initially seeing herself as biracial to eventually fully embracing her identity as a Black woman—a transformation ignited by the tragic murder of George Floyd and her collegiate experiences. It was her college friendships—especially with Black friends raised by Black mothers—which unveiled dimensions of lack of privilege that she herself hadn't encountered, having been raised by a White mother.

Tiernan's insight into the nuanced privileges that come with being raised by a White mother, juxtaposed with what it's like to be raised by a Black mother, opened my eyes to new viewpoints. Her words prompted me to reflect on my own upbringing—how life and the way I view myself might have looked very different had I been adopted and raised by White parents, as many Korean adoptees from my era were.

TABLE 10

    Our talk really deepened my understanding of something fairly significant: how the race of our parents, especially when it's different from our own, molds who we are. It shapes not just our sense of identity but also our views on where we fit into the world—all rooted in the experiences we have growing up.

    Tiernan's candid comments opened my eyes to see those around me and myself more clearly. I was starting to think that I wasn't just sharing meals with strangers on this grand journey; I was breaking bread with women who were becoming my greatest teachers.

April 10, 2023

Hey Diary,

I'm kicking off my longest time away from home today, heading to the always-vibrant city of San Francisco! I'm super-excited because it's time for my yearly photo catch-up with the incredibly talented photographer, who I now consider a friend, Wendy K. Yalom. But this trip's got more in store, stretching beyond San Fran for a whole nine days away from home. The thought of being away for that long is a mix of mostly thrilling with a tad bit bittersweet.

In the middle of the packing chaos this morning, I had this deep discussion with a journalist from *Joy Sauce*. It's this awesome space that's all about amplifying the Asian American story. We got really into talking about what it's like to travel the USA as an Asian American woman. It's kind of a unique view, especially in places where I'm the only Asian face around. Makes me wonder if my White friends ever think about stuff like that—being the only one who stands out, you know?

And it's funny, this interview happened just a week after my convo with Tiernan about her life as a biracial woman in the States. It's starting to feel like all these talks I'm having—whether it's with the amazing women I meet on my travels, someone random at the airport, or reporters—they're all weaving into this one big, beautiful tapestry of insights.

Here's to living in joy,

Shari

Wendy and Shari, April 2023

TRAVEL LOG

April 12, 2023

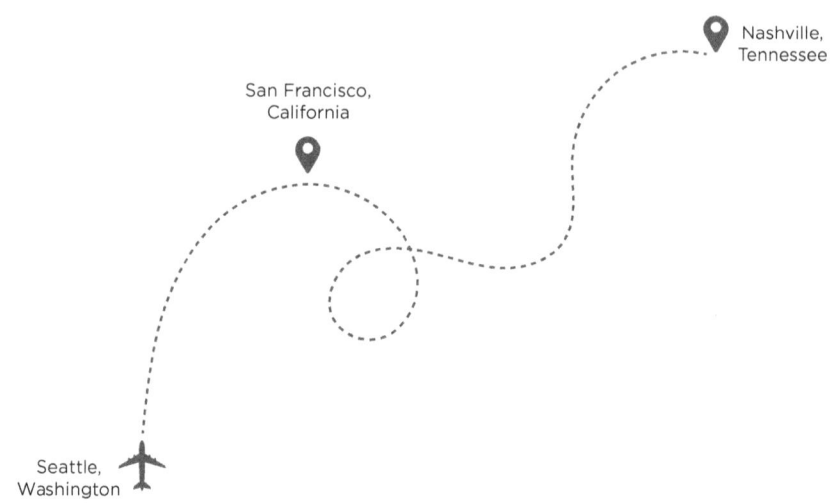

Devin and me at Ella's on 2nd in Nashville, Tennessee

Table 11

Lunch at Ella's on 2nd
Nashville, Tennessee

Devin
Thursday, April 13, 2023—12:00 noon CST

Devin is thirty-nine years old, married for nineteen years. She is a mother of three. She was born and raised in Redding, California, and she is both Japanese and White—identifying as Japanese American. She moved to Nashville, Tennessee from California in September 2020. She is a licensed esthetician who is currently working as a Pre-K teacher and attending school to earn a degree in Child Development.

Today just clicked. Everything fell perfectly into place. I wrapped up a super-fun TV interview on *Today in Nashville*—and wow, I could really get used to that TV studio buzz! There's something about the fast pace, the whirl of activity, and the electric energy of a live broadcast that's just thrilling.

It's been ages since I thought about my first dream back in college: I wanted to be the next Connie Chung. Back then, I didn't quite have the nerve to chase that dream, so I ended up switching my undergrad major from TV journalism to Psychology before moving on to Law School. But here I am now—not exactly Connie Chung, but—at age fifty-three, stepping into the live studio experience that would have astounded my eighteen-year-old self!

I met up with Devin, my second cousin from my adoptive mom's side. We found each other on this warm Spring day under the glow of Nashville's brightly shining sun. It felt like opening a new chapter in a book you know you're going to love. Devin and I have a fourteen-year gap between us and we grew up in different states, so it's not like we had sleepovers or shared secrets growing up. But today, seeing her for the first time in years, with her knockout smile, I felt like maybe I'd been missing out.

She got married when she was just twenty years old, which always seemed so young to me. But listening to her talk about her husband today with such love and devotion, I started to question my own assumptions. Compared to my own rollercoaster of a love life, her marriage seemed as steady as a rock.

Meeting Devin, right on the cusp of her forties—just like Tiernan from Washington—made me pause and think back to my own life at that age. Devin identifies as an introvert, which honestly took me by surprise. She's got a unique energy about her, a vibrant spark that shouts *extrovert*. I wondered if she realized that she has that "it" factor that I can imagine draws people to her. I certainly felt it.

Devin, who recently moved to Nashville from Northern California, is slowly finding her rhythm in this new city—a place that hums with a tune quite different from the laid-back West Coast vibes she's used to. Her kids are blossoming in their new schools, and she's gradually weaving herself into the fabric of this distinctive community. Her teenage years, marked by school changes and constant adaptations to new environments, have given her a certain agility in adjusting to new surroundings. Yet, those same experiences have also taught her to approach things with a level of caution, holding her back from diving in too quickly.

Hearing Devin talk about her relationship with her mother—the challenges and the rebuilding—hit close to home. It felt like she was holding up a mirror, reflecting parts of my own heart that I hadn't dared to examine too closely. Through her story, I began to see the connection between her, her mother (my admired cousin), and my own mom in a new light. I realized

TABLE 11

that I had overlooked some of my mom's qualities, like her strength and resilience. Meeting Devin, her great-niece who undoubtedly carries the same traits, helped me appreciate these qualities in my mother for the first time.

This meeting, coming just a couple of months after my mom passed away, felt like more than just a coincidence. As I drove away, my heart was filled with gratitude for this reminder of the power of unexpected connections, which seem to emerge just when we need them most.

TRAVEL LOG

April 14, 2023

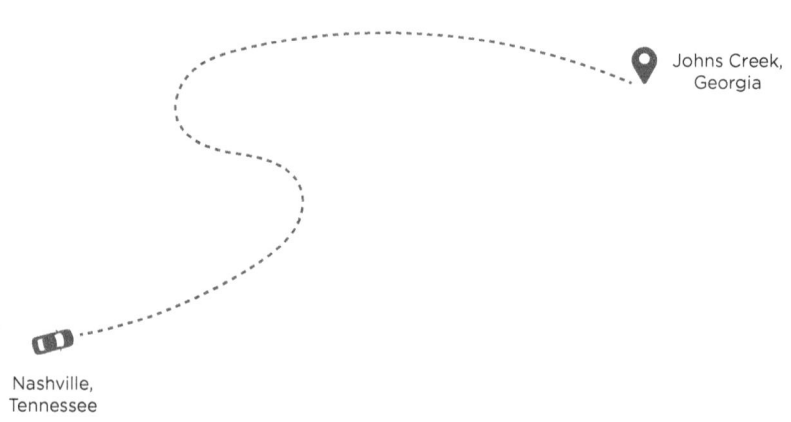

Ashley and me at First Watch in Johns Creek, Georgia

Table 12

Breakfast at First Watch
Johns Creek, Georgia

Ashley
Saturday, April 15, 2023—10:00 AM CDT

Ashley just turned forty the week prior to our meeting. She was born in the Bronx, New York City, but moved with her family at age six to Stone Mountain, Georgia, where she was raised. Her parents immigrated to the United States from Jamaica. Ashley graduated from Columbus State University in Georgia with a BFA in Communications. She is an entrepreneur, a podcaster, and a Digital Marketing Coordinator.

A few years ago, I had the pleasure of being a guest on Ashley's podcast, *The Ash Said It Show*. At the time of our conversation, she was interviewing me via a simple phone call. Most people who know me can attest to my aversion to long telephone calls. But with Ashley, it was different; our conversation flowed effortlessly. Although I've been a guest on several podcasts since, the aura and authenticity Ashley radiated that day remained etched in my memory. So, when my planning began for this ambitious project, I immediately thought of Ashley as one of the women I hoped to meet.

There's a profound wisdom to suggest that there are no coincidences in life.

Our breakfast happened to intersect with a pivotal and stormy season in Ashley's life—a period brimming with both chaos and change. Sitting opposite her in the cozy confines of a popular cafe, I sensed a heaviness in the air, a burden that seemed to cloud her vibrant spirit. As Ashley shared her heart with me, revealing the deep scars left by a toxic workplace that had slowly eroded her soul, I found myself moved by her vulnerability.

I gently suggested, "Maybe this difficult phase is the Universe's way of whispering 'it's time to leave'—a nudge toward escaping a situation that's not just suffocating you but also keeping you from your true path." Reflecting on those words later, I was reminded of a thought shared by Traci from Oregon: "Maybe things happen to lead us to where we truly belong." We're exactly where we need to be.

As we continued to share our lives while devouring the best omelets around, a particular personal story that Ashley told me struck a chord, reflecting back to me glimpses of my own childhood. She talked of the pain of being a kid who just wanted to fit in, yet she was defined as *different* because of her skin color—reduced to "The Black girl." It took me back to my own experience of starting at a new school, where my ethnicity became an unwelcome focal point, obscuring my true identity. I was often referred to as "The Chinese girl" (though, for clarity, I am not Chinese). But Ashley's story delved deeper, as she recounted her move from New York to Stone Mountain, Georgia—a place that held Confederate symbols, which serve as constant reminders of America's troubling past. Yet, in the face of all this, Ashley's spirit remained unbroken. She used her experiences as fuel to empower diverse voices in her work.

Like Ashley, I believe that when faced with a statement such as, "You won't find anyone like you there," the most powerful reply is, "Then that's exactly where I need to be."

TABLE 12

In the gentle warmth of our conversation, I ventured to ask Ashley her thoughts on defining the essence of true friendship. With a thoughtful pause, she shared a nugget of wisdom that resonated deeply: "A real friend," she said, "is someone who, through a lens of love and genuine care, brings the hidden truths to light just when they're needed the most."

And in a moment that felt like the Universe precisely illustrating her point, she leaned in with a smile and softly alerted me to a dab of salad dressing I had unknowingly smeared across my cheek.

April 15, 2023

Dear Diary,

Today was one of those days that kind of sneaks up on you with a surprise that feels just right: making a new friend who's more than you could have ever expected. My chat with Ashley turned into something so much more meaningful than either of us could have imagined.

After we said our goodbyes, Ashley went on her podcast to talk about our meeting. She told her audience about how we met, how things seemed to simply fall right into place, and how something I said—"Let it be easy"—struck a chord with her right when she needed to hear it.

It's funny how sometimes, without even trying, you can say the exact thing someone else needs to hear. Our talk ended up being this beautiful moment of real connection, the kind you can't plan or predict.

It's days like today that make me think about all the people we bump into, whether it's someone we sit next to on a plane or a person we end up talking to while waiting for a coffee. Every one of those meetings feels like it's meant to be—even if it's only for a minute or two.

I've started to really believe that none of these encounters happens by chance. They're all little pieces of something bigger—moments meant for us to share, to learn from, and to keep with us as we go on. I can't help but wonder about the stories and connections tomorrow will bring.

Now, with my rental car packed up, ready for Alabama, I'm positively exhilarated by the thought of dinner with Laura in Huntsville this evening!

Feeling all kinds of excited,

Shari

TRAVEL LOG

April 15, 2023

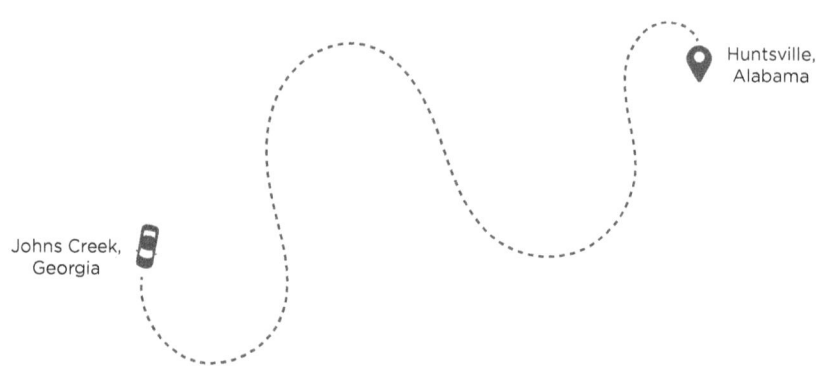

Laura and me at Purveyor in Huntsville, Alabama

Table 13

Huntsville, Alabama
Dinner at Purveyor

Laura
Saturday, April 15, 2023—6:30 PM CDT

Laura is fifty years old and married with two adult children. By the time this book is published, she will have welcomed a daughter-in-law into her family. She was born in Rhode Island, and as the daughter of a career Marine, she grew up in locations all around the country, and even lived for a short time in Iwakuni, Japan. She has resided in Alabama for over twenty-five years and has enjoyed working as a Registered Nurse.

As I was driving to Huntsville, my thoughts drifted back to when Laura and I first crossed paths. It was during a family trip to Southeast Asia, six years ago. Laura's family, with her lively mom, her husband, and their two kids—who were about the same age as mine—seemed like something out of a storybook. But what really caught my attention was Laura's dad. He was a Marine veteran, a navigator from the Vietnam War era. Even though he hadn't served in Vietnam itself, he had a friend who never came back, so being in Vietnam, visiting those historic sites with his family, must have been like closing a circle for him.

Watching Laura's family interact, it was clear they were more than just relatives traveling together; they were best friends on an epic adventure. It was so heartwarming, seeing the kids actually get along, and the grandparents adding their own flavor of wisdom and fun to the mix.

Curious about Laura's own story, I asked her how she met her husband. The sparkle in her eyes as she recounted their blind date was infectious. She was a nursing student, he was seven years her senior, and yet, they clicked right away. They've been together for twenty-seven years now, and he still says it's been "not long enough." That idea, that time flies when you're with the one you love, made me think differently about my own marriage. Could appreciating each other's interests more fully be the key to strengthening our connection?

Despite being Facebook friends with Laura since that brief meeting in Southeast Asia, I didn't know until our dinner at Purveyor that she had undergone open-heart surgery at forty-six years of age. Listening to her talk about her surgery, her recovery, and the lighter moments amidst the challenges—like her mom's comical dash to the hospital, arriving much less pulled together than with her typical stylish flare—reminded me of when I was receiving cancer treatments, pre-pandemic, before the masking era. My husband, who shaves his head, had a cold, so he was required to wear a mask to accompany me to my appointment—looking more like a cancer patient than I did.

Over our dinner conversation, I found so much common ground between Laura and me in the way we view life. We both faced our health scares with determined optimism—wanting to show our kids, and maybe ourselves, that we'd be alright.

The South felt so different from back home in the Pacific Northwest. It was almost like visiting another country, given the distinct cultural differences. While driving to Alabama from Georgia, I'd felt a spiritual reawakening, prompted by the landscape and the conversations around me.

TABLE 13

My time spent in the South was eye-opening, challenging my preconceptions and introducing me to a culture of warmth and acceptance I hadn't fully appreciated before.

And, out of the blue, an invitation came from Birmingham's ABC station 33/40 to be on their morning news show. Their request for me to be on TV there felt like a warm Southern hug, a reminder of the kindness and neighborliness that's still so prevalent across our country.

This road trip gave me a newfound appreciation for the South. How deep and wonderful human connections can be! They can transform us in ways we never expected.

And, just for the record, I found myself falling for the South. Hard.

December 20, **2023**

Dear Diary,

As I edit this manuscript, I wait for my husband to return this evening. I'm serving him with divorce papers. I am including this letter:

Dear _____

I am deeply sorry that our marriage has ended this way. Thank you for providing for our family and supporting me through my health challenges, and through my various attempts at side careers as I raised the children alongside you. I know we each did the best we could, and we were just kids when we started this journey together.

I know things may get very ugly from here as we go through the process of dissolution, because unfortunately financial matters are stressful, and they often get muddy, even for those with the best intentions.

I hope that in the end, our kids will know that we both love them, and that they feel supported by both of us. I hope that we will live the second half of our lives (well, maybe it's the last quarter at this age) with the joy and success that we each deserve. I am grateful for growing up with you. I don't regret marrying you.

Thank you for everything.

With love and respect,

Shari

People talk about twenty-six years of marriage being a long time...and I think back to Laura, in Alabama, whose loving husband describes their twenty-seven years as "not long enough." I wonder if we had held a different mindset throughout our marriage if that would have helped save it.

I want my next spouse—yes, I see myself remarrying—to see our time together as "not long enough." That's my dream.

Feeling hopeful,

Shari

TRAVEL LOG

April 16, 2023

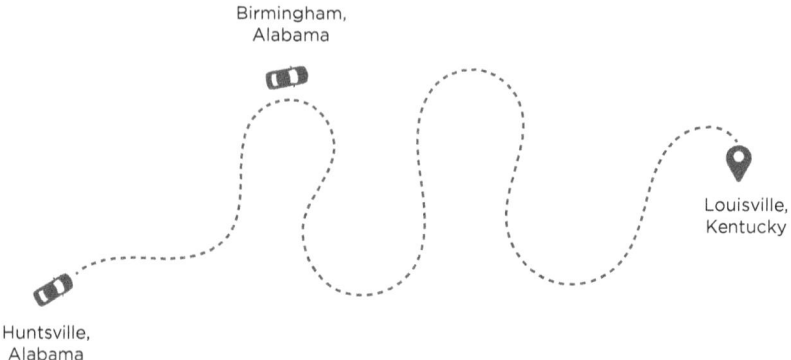

Angie and me at Jeff Ruby's Steakhouse in Louisville, Kentucky

Table 14

Dinner at Jeff Ruby's Steakhouse
Louisville, Kentucky

Angie
Monday, April 17, 2023—6:15 PM EDT

Angie is fifty-one years old, and she has been married for twenty-five years. She and her husband have an adult son who is headed to college this fall. She owns All About Kids, a premier sports center in Louisville, which currently has two locations.

In 2016, Angie and I had a chance meeting overseas. We crossed paths amidst the breathtaking landscapes of South Africa, both embarking on an extraordinary journey with our respective families. When we met, Angie, along with her husband, shared something special with my husband and me: We were all seasoned travelers with the tour company Adventures By Disney, returning to explore new horizons together. Our interactions during that trip were brief and cordial, given the bustling nature of our family-centered activities. Our children were navigating the labyrinth of middle school, so our focus was squarely on cherishing the moments and embracing the richness of this travel experience with our families.

On our South African expedition, we were traveling with various families from all parts of the United States, but Angie and her husband stood out as the only other interracial couple among us. Additionally, her husband Emmitt was one of only three Black individuals in our group—the others being an adult woman from Florida traveling with her elderly father.

Our vacation was made richer by our South African guide, Craig, a White local who shared with us his poignant journey of growing up in the apartheid era. He openly admitted to being raised with racist beliefs, a mindset he was unaware of until a pivotal moment in history. He recounted the powerful transformation he witnessed in his own father during the famous rugby match when Nelson Mandela stepped onto the pitch wearing the Springbok team's traditional green cap and jersey after South Africa's improbable 1995 Rugby World Cup victory. The initial silence in the stadium gave way to a chorus of "Nelson" chants. The guide asked his father if he too had cheered for "Nelson," and with tears in his eyes, his father confessed, "Yes." This narrative left a profound impact on me, sparking thoughts about the potential for change and healing in the face of racial division—not just in South Africa but also back home in the United States.

Coming to Kentucky was akin to arriving in a place like South Africa for me, as it is a state deeply affected by a history of racial injustice. Meeting Angie and her husband Emmitt in this context felt profound. I was aware of the region's historical significance during the Civil War, as it was a place where the North and the South clashed. It filled me with a sense of joy and wonder that, as an Asian woman, I could freely share a meal at an upscale restaurant with my friends who were a mixed-race couple. This was an experience that generations before us could only dream of.

Our choice of restaurant, as Angie had wisely suggested, proved to be nothing short of exceptional. We dined on oysters, followed by hearty meals and good wine. The food and drinks were exquisite, yet what truly set it apart was the welcoming atmosphere and the gracious spirit it exuded. The

TABLE 14

restaurant staff were not just friendly; they radiated happiness. It mirrored Angie's own energy—the very quality I saw draw others to her effortlessly.

Angie's gift for connecting with people and making them feel comfortable resonated deeply with me. It's the way I aspire to show up in the world. Never could I have imagined that one of my role models for acceptance and love would emerge from a chance encounter with a White woman traveling through South Africa with her family—a woman with whom, years later, I would share a meal and befriend—in the southern part of the United States.

Tonight turned out to be one of my most fun nights ever. The energy that Angie and Emmitt together bring to a room was so contagious! And, as a bonus, I now know how to properly pronounce *Louisville!*

TRAVEL LOG

April 18, 2023

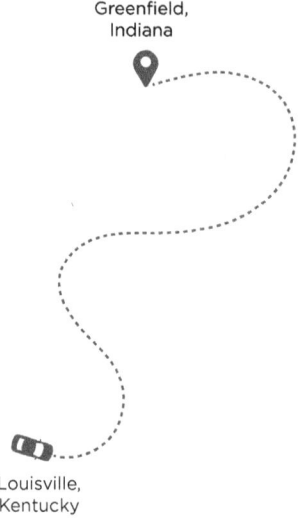

Kristin and me at Hitherto Coffee and Gaming Parlour in Greenfield, Indiana

Table 15

Coffee at Hitherto Coffee and Gaming Parlour Greenfield, Indiana

Kristin
Wednesday, April 19, 2023—10:00 AM EDT

Kristin is thirty-three years old, married, and mom to four young children—the oldest being just seven years of age. She was born in Illinois, and raised in Indiana, which she calls home. She is a web designer and small business owner.

Nearly three years back, in my hunt for the perfect web designer to give my business website a makeover, I stumbled upon Kristin. Her work immediately caught my eye. I'm someone who lives by my calendar, so finding Kristin—who was all about efficiency and being on the same page schedule-wise—was a dream come true.

She immediately understood what I wanted for my site, throwing in her own brilliant ideas—excellent points which hadn't even crossed my mind—and she delivered something better than I'd even hoped for!

When I asked her to be a part of my 50 States Project, her eagerness was the cherry on top. She picked her go-to coffee place for our meetup.

Indiana was new territory for me. I soon learned that calling Indiana "the South" was a mistake—an error not too rare for a Pacific Northwesterner.

Back in high school, my friends and I were regulars at Red Robin restaurant, which was more than just a place to eat; it was our favorite hangout. So, when I heard that Kristin and her husband first met while working at a Red Robin, it was one of those full-circle moments for me.

Kristin is more on the quiet side. She told me that keeping up with friends isn't her strongest suit; that's usually up to them. But she's tight with her family—her husband, their kids, her sister, and her mom. She has a brother whom she is fond of as well, but distance makes their get-togethers rare. I've noticed on this trip that women who are really close with their family members often don't seem to feel the need for a big social circle. It's an interesting pattern that's got me thinking about the link between family connections and friendships.

Our morning chat over coffee and baked goods felt easy, like we were old pals catching up. But the moment that I really cherished was when Kristin mentioned that I was the first Asian person she'd ever had a meal with. It wasn't about her being closed off; it was just simply how things had worked out, given the lack of a significant Asian population where she lives.

In fact, I looked up the demographics. Her current town lists an Asian population of just two percent. It struck me that not only was I the first Asian person Kristin had shared a meal with, but she was also the first person from Indiana with whom I had dined. This is precisely what the 50 States Project is all about: rewriting our personal narratives.

Driving away from our meeting, I felt a swirl of emotions. I was extraordinarily happy and hopeful about the connections I was making.

Now, every time I drive by a Red Robin, I'm going to think of Kristin, and smile.

April 24, **2023**

Dear Diary,

Today was an absolute whirlwind, a pinch-me kind of day. I can hardly believe it, but I was a guest on the *Today Show!* Not just the third hour, mind you, but the second hour—and let me tell you, that's a big deal in the TV world. The entire experience was incredible, and I am positively beaming.

Everyone on the show was really kind—from the producers behind the scenes to the hosts themselves: Al Roker, Sheinelle Jones, Dylan Dreyer, and Craig Melvin. Yes, I was on set with all four hosts! Pinch me: *Al Roker!* They all asked me questions, and they were even gracious enough to take photos with me once my segment concluded. Can you believe it? I'm still on cloud nine.

Sharing my 50 States Project with the whole nation was a dream come true. The journey so far has been nothing short of amazing.

When I returned to my hotel room, it hit me: the flood of messages from strangers asking if I could meet with them in their state. It's overwhelming in the best way possible. I had to take time to absorb it all.

I decided to take a walk to clear my mind. I strolled from my hotel near Rockefeller Plaza all the way to Soho. The commotion of the city swirled around me, and I couldn't help but feel immense joy and gratitude.

With all my heart, I'm determined not to take what has been given to me for granted. I refuse to waste this beautiful life.

With stars in my eyes I am overwhelmed with joy and gratitude.

Simply giddy,

Shari

Meet the Woman on a Mission to Spread Friendship in All 50 States

April 27, 2023

Dear Diary,

Today's a big day—it's my daughter Alexis' birthday!

Alexis has been soaking up the sun and tackling her studies at Lynn University in Boca Raton, Florida, for the past three years. But as this semester wraps up, she's coming home with a big decision in her pocket. She's realized that the traditional four-year college thing might not be her jam, so she's ready to try something different. Watching her figure this out on her own fills me with so much pride.

Our bond is extra special because we share something unique: We were both adopted through Holt International Children's Services. Seeing her grow and navigate life has given me a window into my own past, especially the tricky bits about attachment that followed me around when I was younger. Being her mom is an absolute joy, and I couldn't be prouder of her gutsy move to carve out her own path. I'm all geared up to support her as she shifts gears back to Seattle, ready to start her next adventure.

Living with a mother who's pretty much an open book must be a bit of a challenge for her. My biggest hope is that she will always know just how proud I am of her and how deep my love runs. She wasn't just born; she was born in my heart.

I'm sending her all my love. Happy twenty-third, Lexi! Here's to new beginnings and cherished memories!

Love,

Proud Mom

Happy Birthday, Alexis!

TRAVEL LOG

April 22, 2023

Mai Lara and me at Dons Bogam Wine Bar & BBQ

Table 16

Dinner at Dons Bogam Wine Bar & BBQ
New York City

Mai Lara
Saturday, April 29, 2023—1:00 PM EDT

Mai Lara is a fifty-three-year-old married woman. She and her husband have no children. She works as a freelance consultant in the technology field.

On a rainy afternoon in New York City's Koreatown, I found myself sharing spicy kimchi and laughs with Mai Lara, wrapping up a busy week that was filled with media appearances and business meetings.

Mai Lara, a bit shorter than me—and I'm only a smidge over 5'1"—displays a confidence that's absolutely magnetic, a trait that's dazzled me since our junior year in high school back in 1987. While we saw a lot of each other that year, having friends in common, we attended different high schools, and life sent us spinning into different orbits. Without the threads of social media to tether us, we lost touch. Then, out of the blue, a Facebook notification reeled us back into each other's lives.

Our dinner was like stepping into a time machine—crossing the expanse of years marked by marriages, health battles, and the raw pain of losing our parents. I discovered Mai Lara did not grow up in Seattle as I had assumed. She moved there from Georgia in middle school. The saga of her household, bustling with both biological and adopted siblings—a total of ten children—was the stuff of novels. "We always had enough for two teams," Mai Lara chuckled, sketching a vivid picture of a home brimming with noise and happiness.

The story that really caught my heart was the one about Mai Lara's mom, Betty Tisdale. Imagine this: She got married for the first time at fifty! And that wasn't all. She not only welcomed her new husband's five sons into her life but also teamed up with him to adopt five Vietnamese orphan girls. Mai Lara was the first of the five to be adopted. Together, they created a life centered around love and service, helping other Vietnamese orphans find families too.

Hearing about Betty's adventures in her later years sparked something in me.

As I stepped away from the lively streets of Koreatown, I felt a renewed sense of purpose wash over me. Here I am, in the same life-deciding decade Betty was in when she transformed her own path. It's truly never too late for love to find us, for new paths to open, or to make our mark. It's never too late to make a positive impact in the world. Betty Tisdale's remarkable life after fifty reminded me of the unfolding chapters of my own life. I was excited to think that the most life-changing and rewarding parts of our journey can start when we least expect it.

TRAVEL LOG

Cindy and me at Halls Chophouse

Table 17

Dinner at Halls Chophouse
Greenville, South Carolina

Cindy
Friday, May 5, 2023—5:00 PM EDT

Cindy is a fifty-seven-year-old woman married to a man of Creole descent. She was born in Seattle, Washington and raised in Portland, Oregon. She has been married for seventeen years. While having no biological children, her husband has two adult sons. She moved to Greenville, South Carolina in 2010. Cindy is a successful entrepreneur, co-owner of several med spa businesses.

On a stormy day in Seattle, Cindy's life took a turn that would shape her future in the most unexpected way. As she sat stuck in traffic, inching her way across Seattle's 520 floating bridge, with waves crashing over its sides, a great sense of unease swept over her. This was more than just a troublesome commute; it was a dangerous situation. In that moment, Cindy picked up her phone and called her husband, delivering a declaration that would change their lives forever. She told him it was time to look for a job elsewhere, because she was ready to make a move.

Her husband, who has Southern roots, shared her sentiment. They both yearned for a change of scenery, a new chapter in a different part of the country. Without hesitation, he began scouring job listings outside of Washington State—and fate led him to Greenville, South Carolina.

At first, Cindy held onto her job in Seattle, working remotely and making monthly cross-country trips to meet her team in person. It was a demanding routine that stretched on for three long years. Then, one day, her husband posed a question that caused her to reevaluate her life: "Are you ready to put down roots?"

This question struck a chord. It made her pause and reflect. Putting down roots meant more than just establishing social connections; it also meant anchoring her career. She took the leap. From that moment on, Greenville became more than just her physical home—it became her emotional anchor. Cindy decided it was time to create something meaningful and lasting.

And that's precisely what she did. Cindy co-founded an aesthetics medical spa, Back to 30, with a partner—a venture that proved to be incredibly successful. Over the years, they expanded to four locations, and, a decade after opening their first establishment, they formed a partnership with a national corporation.

Cindy's journey inspired me to reflect on the concept of planting roots—both physical and emotional. As someone who was adopted and abandoned as a baby, I have always felt like I've lacked roots, without a sense of belonging and identity. It had never occurred to me that I could take steps to create my own roots.

As I continued in my travels across the country, I decided to make a conscious effort to identify the places that resonate with me on a profound level. In each encounter with the women I met, I was paying close attention to the qualities I admire—the qualities I hope to find in the friendships I want to cultivate and nurture. Witnessing Cindy's transformation since she chose to plant roots instilled in me a newfound motivation and excitement for my own future.

I now understood that even as a foundling, I, too, can have roots.

TABLE 17

    I couldn't help but wonder if I needed to put down roots not only in the space where I live, but also at home with my husband. Had I ever done that? It seemed to me that I had; but after talking with Cindy, I decided that when I got back home, I would tell him that I'm choosing to put down roots in our relationship—something I'd never said out loud to anyone.

May 6, 2023

Dear Diary,

I've been reflecting a lot on my marriage—the good and the increasingly troubling. Home doesn't feel like home these days. My husband and I, we've been arguing more than ever. I feel an unease in returning home now, a growing sense of disconnection. I'm feeling the angst in my stomach every time I board a plane headed for home. I wonder if my gut knows what my head isn't ready to accept. We've been together for twenty-eight years—nearly twenty-six of those as a married couple. Yet it feels like we're a world apart.

The core of our problem, in my opinion, is alcohol abuse. My husband currently won't acknowledge it, but his drinking is what we are fighting constantly about, and I feel it is destroying our marriage. I've been coping with this feeling for years. And now, seeing our daughter—who is back from college and living at home—struggle alone with similar experiences with her dad while I'm away—plus the confrontations between my husband and me every time I return—it's overwhelming.

Divorce is a heart-wrenching thought, one I can barely entertain. But I'm at a crossroads. I'm pleading with him to seek help, willing to do anything to salvage our marriage. Being away has given me clarity, an unobscured view of our reality.

Contemplating what is ahead,

Shari

Christmas Eve, **2023**

Dear Diary,

It's been four days since I served my husband with divorce papers. This Christmas Eve, I'm living my absolute best life, and it feels fabulous. No apologies, no regrets—just pure, unadulterated joy. For the first time ever, I'm doing Christmas my way, surrounded by my two incredible kids and our two full-of-energy dogs.

Gone are the days of conforming to holiday expectations that didn't spark joy in my soul. This year, it's all about crafting our own traditions, making memories that we'll treasure forever. And let me tell you, the vibe is electric. I'm so filled with happiness. I've found myself spontaneously dancing and singing around the house!

Facing the prospect of losing a lot no longer scares me. Why? Because in this moment, I've never felt more empowered—more alive. It's a reminder that sometimes, when it feels like you're about to lose everything, you're actually discovering what truly matters.

So, here's to personal power, to choosing joy, and to spending Christmas Eve exactly how we want. Today isn't just a holiday for me. It's a declaration of my ability to find happiness on my own terms.

Cheers to that!

Shari

TRAVEL LOG:

May 6, 2023

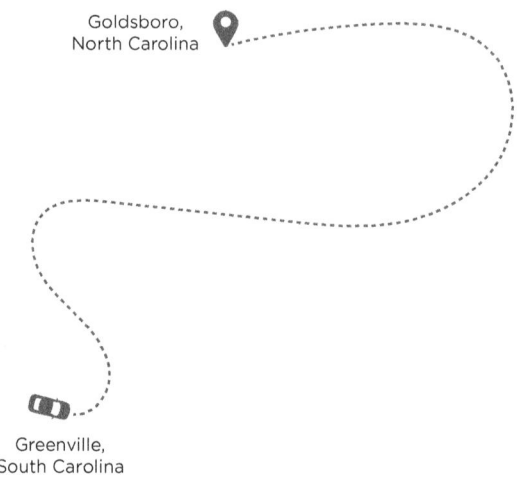

Melissa and me at The Laughing Owl in Goldsboro, North Carolina

Table 18

Dinner at The Laughing Owl
Goldsboro, North Carolina

Melissa
Saturday, May 6, 2023—6:00 PM EST

Melissa was born and raised in North Carolina. She is fifty-three years old, married, with three adult daughters. She has worked as a school teacher and she is currently a podcaster.

When I reflected upon my evening spent with Melissa, the first two words that came to mind are *kind* and *brave*.

I knew Melissa was looking forward to our meeting; she made me feel welcome through her Instagram posts and her kind sharing of my journey as our date approached. She even generously highlighted some of my media appearances—an act of goodwill that truly touched my heart. It was this thoughtful gesture that made me slightly nervous before our meeting, something I hadn't experienced with my previous meetings. I couldn't pinpoint the source of my anxiety, but I found myself wondering if Melissa and I would be able to connect on a meaningful level. Perhaps I was afraid she would feel disappointed if our meeting did not live up to her expectations.

As it turned out, my worries were unfounded. When we finally met, she instantly made me feel at home, surprising me with bespoke gifts that were made and curated by her with the help of her close friends. We shared a wonderfully delicious dinner at a popular Asian–American fusion restaurant— where we had the nicest young server, who was as friendly as can be.

Melissa brought up her Enneagram number. The Enneagram, I have come to learn, is a system for understanding personality types. Many people find it helpful for self-awareness and personal growth. Melissa proudly declared her dominant Enneagram number to be 2, and she emphatically asserted that she embodied every aspect of that number. Curious, I researched the traits of a 2, and I couldn't help but agree with Melissa wholeheartedly. A 2 is often referred to as "The Helper." They are known for their kindness, generosity, warm-heartedness, and capacity for love when at their best. They are inherently motivated by a deep-seated desire to be of assistance to others. Even without knowledge of her Enneagram number, this is exactly how I would have described Melissa.

During our dinner conversation, Melissa and I discovered that we are about the same age. I couldn't resist asking her about her experience of being a woman in her fifties. She revealed that, like me, she had decided to embrace life to the fullest once she hit this milestone decade.

Melissa has resolved to say *yes* more often to things that push her outside of her comfort zone. She regaled me with a perfect example of how she's doing just that. To celebrate her fiftieth birthday, she decided to face one of her deepest fears: ziplining. Melissa described trembling like a leaf while harnessed and standing on the zipline platform; but despite her apprehension, she took the leap. She jokingly mentioned that she had offered a quick prayer just before taking off from the platform: "Well, if I die, let me go quick!"

I felt an overwhelming sense of sisterly pride, realizing that her ziplining adventure symbolized all the incredible feats she can and will achieve in her fifties and beyond.

TABLE 18

Melissa's adventures didn't end there. In 2022, she embarked on her first flight since her college days, a span of more than thirty years. She traversed the country—a journey that was a first for her—to visit one of her daughters who resides in Pasadena, California.

I was struck by the beautiful irony that I had entered our meeting uncertain if Melissa and I would connect, only to discover that we were both embracing our fifties in remarkably similar ways. After dinner, we took a fun walk through the historic streets of Goldsboro, taking photos in front of fabulous art pieces and even stopping to play an outdoor piano.

I was deeply inspired by Melissa's unwavering determination to confront her fears head-on. Our dinner conversation reminds me of how important it is to take that leap—(literally)—and enjoy the view!

TRAVEL LOG

May 7, 2023

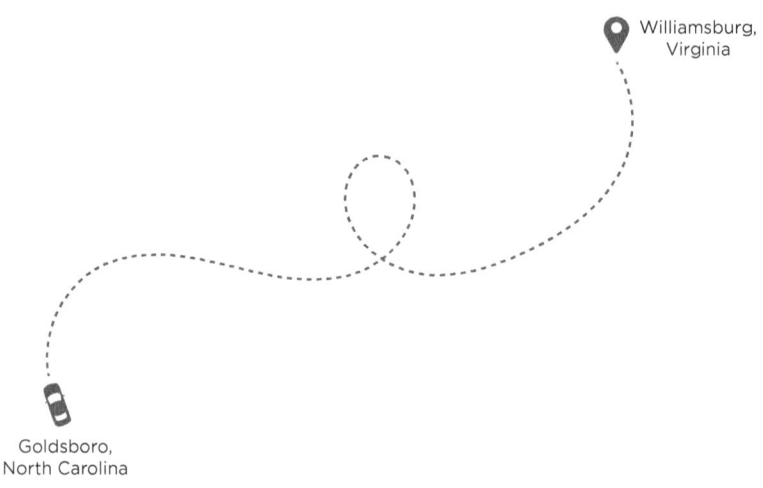

Megan and me at The Amber Ox Public House, Williamsburg, Virginia

Table 19

Dinner at The Amber Ox Public House Williamsburg, Virginia

Megan
Sunday, May 7, 2023—4:30 PM EDT

Megan is forty years old, married for sixteen years. She and her husband are parents to a grade-school-aged daughter. She grew up in Northern Virginia, and after living on the West Coast for several years, she moved to Williamsburg just this past year. She is a small business owner working as a makeup artist.

I found myself in Williamsburg without having delved into the particulars of the neighborhood where Megan suggested we meet. I switched my lodging at the last minute, to a hotel within walking distance of Megan's chosen restaurant. Little did I know, this twist of fate would lead me to the heart of Colonial Williamsburg, where history was not merely preserved but animated with vibrant authenticity.

As I strolled from my hotel to our meeting point, I couldn't help but smile at the sights that unfolded before me. Many of the shop owners were dressed in Colonial attire, horse-drawn carriages traversed the cobblestone streets, and living history exhibits with convincing actors greeted passersby. It felt as though I had unwittingly stepped onto a movie set. The whole neighborhood displayed a charm so enchanting, I had to stop and take several photos on my way to the restaurant. What a loss it would have been had I not changed hotels! I was so glad I hadn't missed this chance to immerse myself in the living history of Williamsburg during my brief visit.

The place Megan chose for us was a modern pub that boasted of locally sourced ingredients—a yummy nod to the present in this historic town.

Megan and I uncovered some remarkable coincidences during our time together. It turned out that Megan's mother-in-law is from Bainbridge Island, Washington—the island that is located just a thirty-minute ferry ride from Seattle, where my mother was born. Another coincidence: Both of Megan's parents were graduates of the University of Illinois Urbana–Champaign—the very same institution that my father proudly called his alma mater. These serendipitous connections left me with a profound sense that Megan and I were meant to cross paths and share our stories.

Growing up with my adoptive parents' distinctly Japanese-sounding surname—Aoyama—I often found myself engaged in debates with strangers around my identity. I was adopted from South Korea, of full Korean heritage—not Japanese. Even in my preschool years, I recall arguing with adults—including an elderly Japanese gentleman in a dentist's waiting room. I recall a similar disagreement with a teacher during my kindergarten days, who insisted that I was wrong in my assertion that I am Korean. The name *Aoyama* always felt foreign to me. So, since early childhood, I knew that if I ever got married, I intended to change my last name.

Drawing upon my own experiences, I asked Megan about the choices we make regarding our surnames. Her husband's last name is of Japanese origin—a detail that could invite assumptions and preconceptions about Megan. However, Megan candidly shared that while it has not posed a personal dilemma for her, she has encountered intriguing reactions and expectations based solely on her married name.

TABLE 19

She recounted a humorous anecdote from her career as a makeup artist, where she's often found herself the favored choice for Asian clients, predicated on the misconception that her surname confers a unique expertise in enhancing Asian features. While Megan's talents are unquestionable, they stem from her innate aptitude and dedicated learning, rather than from her ethnic background. Some clients, well-intentioned yet misinformed, have even ventured to comment, "I can see it"—referring to Asian features they are desperately searching her face to find, solely because of her last name! In truth, Megan has no Asian heritage in her lineage—no Asian features! She laughed and mused, "People see what they're looking for."

Her statement would become my constant reminder: I have the power to look at the world and decide how I'm going to view it.

TRAVEL LOG

May 14, 2023

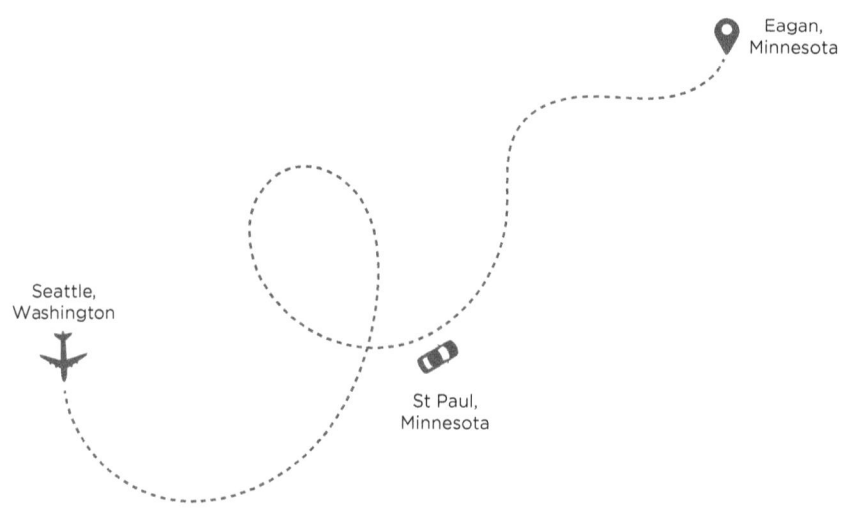

Ann and me at the Omni Viking Lakes Hotel, Eagan, Minnesota

Table 20

Dinner at Ember & Ice, the Omni Viking Lakes Hotel Eagan, Minnesota

Ann
Monday, May 15, 2023—6:00 PM CDT

Ann is sixty-one years old, and she has been married to her college sweetheart for thirty-two years. She and her husband have no children. Ann was born and raised in Wisconsin and then moved to Minnesota for college—which has been her home ever since. Ann is the president of a non-profit serving senior citizens and their families.

Meeting Ann was like finding a book you didn't even know you needed, only to be completely hooked by the first chapter. Steve, our mutual friend, was the link between us. He and I bonded as prior law-school classmates and co-workers. Ann and Steve's friendship went back even further than ours to their college days, where they ran around with the same group of friends. Steve, learning through a Facebook post that I was looking for a woman in Minnesota to connect with for this project, quickly referred me to Ann.

Over dinner, Ann shared that after years of hustling in the corporate world, she made a surprising jump to lead a non-profit—a move as unexpected as any plot twist. This wasn't just any organization, but one dedicated to transforming the idea of aging from a *burden* into a *celebration*—a cause which became deeply meaningful to her. She stumbled upon the group during a vulnerable time: Her father had begun to lose his memories. Her respect for their work morphed into deeper involvement. She evolved from a donor to a board member, and finally became its president in 2015.

For our rendezvous, Ann chose a restaurant that represented Minnesota's Viking spirit. We shared a charcuterie board complemented by glasses of red wine.

Our conversation drifted into deep waters, touching on race—a topic that's often as precarious as walking a tightrope. Yet, it unfolded with surprising ease, turning into one of the most open and profound discussions I'd ever had on the subject. Ann shared her personal journey toward understanding, shaped by her experiences. She was determined to move beyond her small-town Wisconsin upbringing. Her empathy and insights struck a chord, especially when she addressed the pressure I felt as an Asian American to always represent my race in a positive light. "That shouldn't be your burden to carry," she told me, and her words resonated deeply.

Since then, I've often thought about what she said and quietly wondered, *What choice do I have?*

Among the many stories we exchanged, a favorite of mine was Ann's story about an elderly man who had been absent from his weekly senior shuttle-bus outing due to illness. There was collective joy upon his return. Everyone expressed how much they missed him. In Ann's words, "Everyone wants to know they are missed."

I agreed with her. I decided after our encounter that I wanted to aspire to live so that my absence is felt when I'm gone. Maybe, one day, my epitaph will read, "She lived in such a powerful way, that the world feels her absence." This simple sentence encapsulates how I hope to have an impact upon the people I meet.

TRAVEL LOG

May 16, 2023

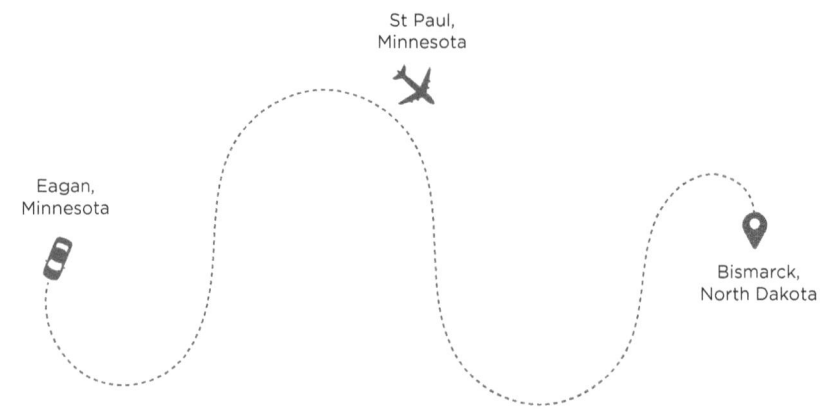

Linda and me at the Broadway Grill & Tavern, Bismarck, North Dakota

Table 21

Wine at Broadway Grill & Tavern
Bismarck, North Dakota

Linda
Tuesday, May 16, 2023—7:00 PM CDT

Linda is yet another woman in my 50 States Project who is in a milestone year: She just turned sixty years old. She has been married for thirty-eight years, with four adult daughters. She was born and raised in North Dakota, where she became a very active stay-at-home mom.

As I walked into the sizeable, bustling Broadway Grill & Tavern restaurant, my eyes were instantly drawn to the lively bar, where Linda was waving me over with a warm smile. She was deep in conversation with an old high-school friend who, by an amazing coincidence, also knew the mutual friend who had introduced us. This moment perfectly captured the tight-knit community vibe of Bismarck—a place where familiar faces and connections seem woven into the very fabric of the town.

My familiarity with the Dakotas was pretty slim before this trip. It surprised me to learn that the entire population of the state of North Dakota is on par with the city of Seattle! My hotel happened to be situated next to the Germans from Russia Heritage Society, sparking the start of my dive into the state's rich history of German immigration in the early 1900s. Linda, sharing stories over drinks, told me about her grandparents, who were among those Germans from Russia who made their way to America.

Our connection grew as we discovered our mutual passions for international travel and for the joys of deep friendship. Linda's effervescent personality made our conversation flow seamlessly, especially when we touched on our families' contributions during WWII and the military service of the generations that followed. I've always been moved by the stories of immigrant families who send their sons (and now daughters) to defend America's freedoms. It's a poignant reminder of the beauty of America, where we can choose to embrace our dual identities—our American citizenship and our ancestral heritage.

I fell in love with the communal spirit that Bismarck radiates. I couldn't have asked for a better guide to the heart of this city than Linda. She made me realize that if I ever decide to move, I might opt for a smaller place rather than a bustling metropolis like Seattle—settling in a smaller city or town where walking into a restaurant or a store means always seeing a familiar face.

Maybe home is a place where a friendly *hello* can be found around every corner.

TRAVEL LOG

May 17, 2023

Toni and me at her home in Rapid City, South Dakota

Table 22

Dinner at Toni's Home
Rapid City, South Dakota

Toni
Wednesday, May 17, 2023—7:00 PM MDT

Toni is sixty-one years old, born and raised in South Dakota. She is not married. While she has no children of her own, she comes from a large family, with many nieces, nephews, and even grandnieces. She currently works as a paralegal.

Driving from Bismarck to Rapid City felt like being stuck reading the same page of a book for five hours straight—the landscape barely shifting except for an occasional curve or dip in the road. It was one of those drives where you start questioning whether you're moving at all. It felt like the world outside was just spinning in a loop. I even took a few photos trying to capture the monotony, but each shot looked pretty much the same. Unless you really squinted.

But the trip was worth it. Toni's life seemed straight out of a heartwarming novel, brimming with outdoor escapades and family ties that sounded almost too perfect. She spoke of her father with such warmth and admiration, it was clear she was still trying to find her way without him. Her stories of water sports, camping, and gardening drew a vivid picture of a childhood rich with real-life adventures, from a time before smart phones and social media.

Toni had invited me over for dinner, and since we were connected through a mutual friend, I felt comfortable heading to her place. I'm so glad I did. Her home was a rich reflection of her passions. In addition to personal keepsakes, her place also had a camera set up in front of a large picture window, ready for that perfect shot—just the right nod to the beauty of the area that she has decided to call home. That night, I discovered Toni's love for bird watching. To my surprise, it piqued my interest too. After I left, I even bought a beginner's guide to birding, eager to see what had her so hooked.

Her home was a serene sanctuary, with wide-open views that made me feel connected to the world outside. It was a space where you could watch the day slowly unfold and feel completely at peace. Everything about it mirrored Toni—open, natural, and effortlessly authentic. It reminded me of the time I visited Anna in Arizona—another place that felt perfectly in tune with its owner.

Toni offered me homemade raspberry wine, and despite my initial reservations, I discovered that it was fantastic. I've been singing praises of that wine ever since, searching everywhere for a taste that could match that unique flavor. Nothing has come close.

This visit made me reflect once again on the idea of home, and where I envision myself settling. The hustle and bustle of massive cities like New York is thrilling; yet the tranquility of the countryside—the room to breathe and the chance to cultivate a garden—pulls at me in ways I can't dismiss. Toni's choice to move back to South Dakota after years away struck a chord with me. It's like those migratory birds she adores—always returning to the place that feels right, no matter the distance they've flown.

I found myself thinking about my own living space, wondering if making it truly mine, truly me—like Toni and Anna have accomplished—could be the key to feeling at home. Perhaps, I thought, it's not so much the location, but how we fill it—so that our space feels in tune with our heart.

February 10, **2024**

Dear Diary,

As I know now, finding a place that truly feels like home isn't just about the size of the plot or how perfectly the interior is decorated. I've learned that the hard way. We poured money and effort into remodeling our family house just three years ago. It's stunning—really, it is—reflecting my personal style with every color choice and design detail. Yet, somehow, it still hasn't felt quite right.

It turns out, it wasn't the space itself. The real issue was the couple living in it.

As I think about moving on, I'm starting to see how crucial it is to look beyond the aesthetics of the structure. When I share my space with my next someone, I'm going to make sure that he feels like home.

Reflecting,

Shari

TRAVEL LOG

May 19, 2023

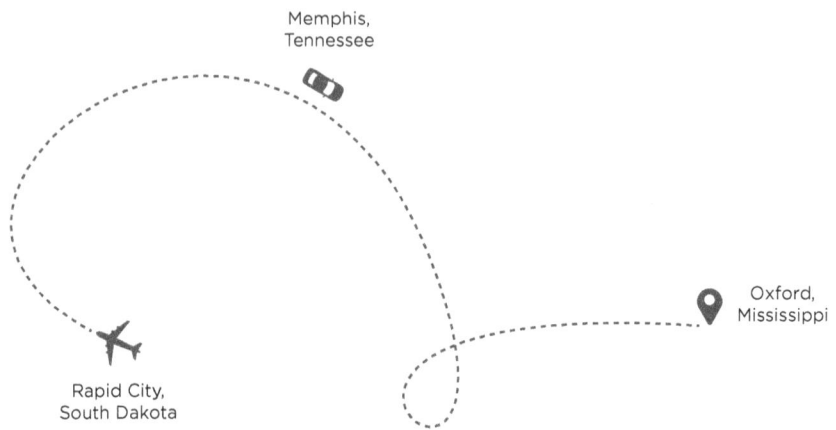

Keli and me at Heartbreak Coffee Roasters, Oxford, Mississippi

Table 23

Coffee at Heartbreak Coffee Roasters
Oxford, Mississippi

Keli
Sunday, May 21, 2023—8:00 AM CDT

Keli is forty-nine years old, born and raised in Mississippi. She and her husband met as college students at Ole Miss, and they have been married for twenty-four years. They have three daughters. Their oldest is the same age as my son, who turned twenty-one this year. She is an attorney who now owns her own business working as a photographer and branding specialist.

I touched down in Memphis, Tennessee, departing from Rapid City, South Dakota. My initial impression of Memphis was one of sorrow, as the city appeared worn and in decline. Thankfully, I heeded the advice of my friend, AJ, who is from Memphis, not to stay as a single woman traveler alone in Memphis, due to safety concerns, especially given my unfamiliarity with the area. I had been forewarned about the city's struggles with violence, so I proceeded cautiously as I headed towards Mississippi. Some research revealed that Memphis currently ranks as one of the most dangerous cities in the country. As I drove through, my heart ached for this city steeped in history, and I hoped it would find a way to rejuvenate itself.

Crossing the state line into Mississippi, the scenery underwent an instant transformation. The drive from the *Welcome to Mississippi* highway sign to Oxford felt especially hospitable. For nearly an hour, lush greenery surrounded me, creating a tranquil and peaceful atmosphere.

Besides the picturesque landscape, I couldn't help but notice several grand estates along the way, arousing my curiosity about life in this part of Mississippi.

Although I had heard of Ole Miss—who hasn't seen the beloved Sandra Bullock film, *The Blind Side?*—I had only a basic picture of the university's rich culture and legacy. It wasn't until I set foot in Oxford that I truly grasped its allure and spirit, which was contagious.

Keli suggested we meet at a coffee shop in Oxford Square, conveniently located near Ole Miss. I decided to stay nearby, unaware that it was graduation weekend for both the university and local high schools. The neighborhood was pulsing with the positive vibes of families and friends.

With an extra day to spare in Oxford, I explored the historic square. I texted my husband, jokingly suggesting we could retire in Oxford, Mississippi—a town known as the "Velvet Ditch" for its comfortable allure that keeps people from ever wanting to leave. It boasts a unique blend of culture, history, art, and vibrancy that's truly special.

I was excited to meet Keli, grateful that she was making time for me during such a busy weekend. As a photographer, she had worked a wedding the previous day, and she had upcoming graduation events for one of her daughters *on* that very day! But she was generous enough to meet up with me that morning.

We hit it off immediately over coffee and shared a lot of laughs. Keli is the type of person I'd naturally strike up a conversation with at a social event. Our shared sense of humor was evident as we spent the morning swapping stories and laughing, including a hilarious discussion about watermelons. While setting up my phone to record a video with Keli, I mentioned that a woman I met in California, Hannah, a voice instructor, had suggested saying

TABLE 23

the word *watermelon* in silent videos to show social interactions, because the way the mouth forms the word is visually interesting. Keli burst into laughter and shared that her hometown of Water Valley is famous for its annual Watermelon Carnival, complete with seed-spitting contests.

Fitness and healthy living are important to Keli and her family. Her husband is a former professional athlete. I shared with her my challenges with fitness and health while traveling for my 50 States Project. My suitcases are always packed with health bars, vitamins, exercise equipment, and even a travel scale to ensure that I stay as healthy as possible.

Keli and her husband, both Mississippi natives, have chosen to raise their family in the state they grew up in, just as my husband and I did in Washington. Travel has been a fundamental part of our child-rearing experiences, as we wanted to expose our kids to new people, places, and cultures. Every year, Keli's family eagerly anticipates their annual two-week RV trip, selecting a new part of the country to explore. I shared that my husband and I have embarked on international travels with our children—each year exploring a new country.

Because of the 50 States project, I've discovered that simply traveling within the United States feels like exploring at least fifty different countries! Each state has its own unique culture.

Many aspects of my meeting with Keli have stayed with me since we parted ways. Our common interests, educational background, entrepreneurial spirit, and similar styles naturally drew me to her. As we said our goodbyes, I couldn't help but think, "I could definitely see myself going on a girls' trip with Keli."

However, it wasn't our similarities that lingered in my thoughts; it was our differences that stayed on my mind. Keli is actively involved in her church. I used to put up defensive walls when I learned someone was a member of an organized religion. These walls stemmed from my strict religious upbringing, which caused me to harbor resentment against anything that sounded like organized religion, for a significant portion of my adult life. Meeting women across the South who are deeply committed to their faith and their church has given me a new perspective. Witnessing their love for their faith and their families has helped me appreciate the benefits of such a commitment.

The best thing that I've noticed in all these shared meals is that our differing beliefs don't hinder our ability to forge friendships and enjoy each other's company. My experience with Keli was no exception. I felt a spiritual shift going on inside of me during these travels, which I had not expected.

While I began this project looking for what I had in common with the women I was planning to meet, I was finding out that what makes us different is really where the beauty lies.

TRAVEL LOG

June 2, 2023

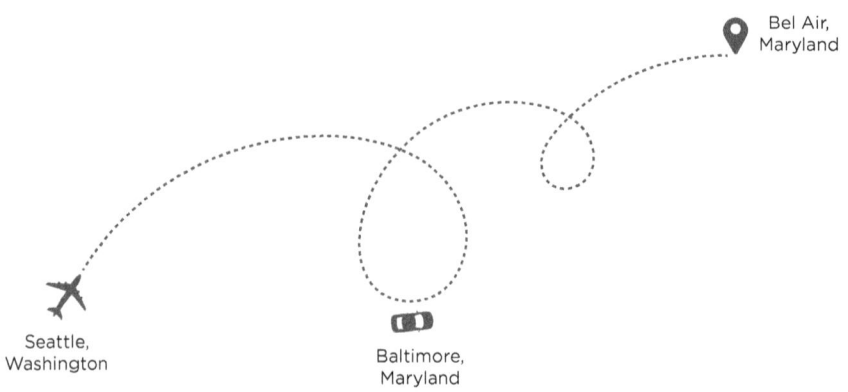

Carrie and me at Barrett's on the Pike, Bel Air, Maryland

Table 24

Brunch at Barrett's on the Pike
Bel Air, Maryland

Carrie
Saturday, June 3, 2023—11:00 AM, EDT

Carrie is fifty-four years old, married for twenty-four years. She is a mom to three adult sons. She was born in Florida and has called Maryland home for over thirty years. She runs operations for Capucia Publishing, my fabulous publishing house.

For over three years, Carrie and I were like two planets orbiting the same star, working together yet never crossing paths in person—until today. This morning, I woke up filled with a mix of excitement and curiosity. I was finally going to meet the person who's been my behind-the-scenes hero as I've published my three-volume *Friendship Series*. Carrie, with her magic touch, has been the expert in bringing my books to life—nurturing them from mere ideas to real books that sit on real shelves and inspire my readers.

Sitting across from Carrie at a comfy spot for brunch, I felt like I was sharing a meal with an old friend rather than meeting a work colleague for the first time. Over eggs and toast in the bustling restaurant, we quickly dived into swapping tales of family life and personal adventures. I was eager to learn about Carrie's college days, imagining her immersed in literature or journalism studies. Yet, Carrie's revelation that she never finished college took me by surprise. She's a testament to the power of self-education, as she has shaped her own career in the publishing world without a degree to her name.

Growing up, the idea of *not* going to college never even flickered across my mind. My parents had etched the college route so deeply into my childhood expectations that I used to dream that my college fund was a bottomless treasure chest. I often asked my parents for the things that I saw other kids receive—like a swing set or a kiddie pool—but I was always gently reminded that funds were being funneled into my future education. While I left college debt-free, thanks to my parents' sacrifices, meeting Carrie confirmed what I have witnessed time and time again: There are many roads to success, and not all of them are paved through college campuses.

Carrie's entry into publishing began unconventionally. She joined a community group known affectionately as "The Driveway Moms." A serendipitous connection within this circle led her to a role that blossomed into the directorship of operations for Capucia Publishing and its affiliate author-coaching enterprise. Her story is a poignant reminder that sometimes, life's most fulfilling opportunities sprout from the least expected places.

As we exchanged laughter and stories over brunch, I found myself pondering the fortuitous twists that had led us here—to a cozy table in Bel Air, Maryland. We were more than just colleagues; we were kindred spirits, each following our unique, sometimes winding road, yet crossing here, in this moment. Carrie had navigated her way into publishing via an unexpected means. And I had stumbled into writing without any formal training. There we were, briefly intertwined on this delightful and unpredictable journey.

For me, our brunch became more than just a meeting. It was a celebration of life's spontaneous encounters—a testament to the value of embracing every unforeseen twist and turn with open arms.

June 7, **2024**

Dear Diary,

We sold our family home within only thirty-six hours of listing it, and then I had a mad scramble to find a rental with enough room for Alexis, Zach, and our two loving Labrador dogs, Nitro and Thunder. Even though my kids are young adults, ready to launch, I felt strongly that they needed a landing pad—a place they could always stay while navigating their next moves toward independence.

My ex decided to rent a one-bedroom apartment, so the responsibility falls on me to provide a place for the kids and the dogs to land. Fortunately, I found a one-year rental. The curb appeal isn't great, but I'm looking forward to seeing what I can do with the inside space. It will serve its purpose, and it's closer to the man I'm dating and to my friends.

And, to add to all the changes, just a couple of days ago, Zach received a great job offer from Columbia University's medical center in New York! He's moving to New York to start his first job out of college in just a few weeks. So we're scrambling now to find housing for him.

It's been nearly six months since my first date with this man I'm spending more and more time with, and he played a big role in my decision to find a rental home in the area. Just this morning, I was texting my college roommate, Melissa, wondering if I should talk to him about our future—or if it's too early. With all the changes in my life right now, I'm feeling more vulnerable than usual, and it's uncomfortable.

However, today, while going through the first formal round of edits on my book manuscript, I revisited my time with Carrie in Maryland. At the end of that chapter, I reread my words about life's twists and turns and how I wanted to embrace them with open arms. That is truly how I want to move forward in this next chapter of my life!

So, I'm not going to have a conversation with him about our unknown future or intentions right now. Instead, I'm going to focus on the present, appreciating the beauty and unexpected lessons of this journey.

I'm thankful for the fifty strangers I met who have become not just my friends, but my teachers.

Embracing life,

Shari

TRAVEL LOG

June 3, 2023

Anne and me at The Clubhouse in Millsboro, Delaware

Table 25

Dinner at The Clubhouse
Millsboro, Delaware

Anne
Saturday, June 3, 2023—6:00 PM EDT

Anne is fifty-six years old. She was born and raised in Westchester County, New York, and moved to Delaware in 2021 after calling Greenwich, Connecticut her home for over thirty years. She is the owner of a PR and marketing firm, Danika Communications.

Two years into her big move to Delaware, Anne is still finding her footing. Over our shared dinner, she recounted memories of her life in Greenwich—with its familiar streets in the comforting shadow of her childhood home in Westchester County. These memories hold a special place in her heart that Millsboro hasn't quite managed to occupy yet. Despite her efforts to weave herself into the fabric of her new community—even joining the local Community Association Board in an attempt to root herself deeper—Millsboro still feels more like a big sweater that hasn't quite shrunk to fit.

    I got to visit Anne at her new place, where we decided to eat at one of the expansive property's clubhouses, with a spectacular view of the gardens and grounds. It was lovely seeing where she lives, and the salads we ordered were huge—making it a perfect setting for our animated conversation.

Meeting Anne felt like destiny, even though our families moved in totally different circles. We discovered that we were both only children, each deeply connected to our father, and that we had each lost our dad in our thirties. Losing our dads turned our world upside down, leaving us to care for our moms on our own.

My mom moved in with my family for a few years after my dad passed, while Anne's mom moved from Florida to be closer to her in Connecticut. As Anne talked about the mix of love and frustration in her relationship with her mom, I felt a deep connection. We both shared the experience of being cherished by our father as an only child, and navigating a more complicated relationship with our mother.

Our paths crossing felt like a little nudge from the Universe, especially given the timing. The original plan for my Delaware visit fell apart when the woman I was supposed to meet jetted off on a surprise trip, leaving me scrambling. But then, as if by magic, a connection through a friend in Seattle brought Anne into my life. If this 50 States Project has taught me anything, it's to trust in the journey—to believe that the right people will appear at the right time. And just like that, a last-minute social media plea connected me with Anne.

After our chat, Anne sent me a text that felt like a hug through the phone, saying how much our conversation made her think, shifting something deep inside her. I'd felt the same stirrings. She left me with words that echoed long after our shared meal came to an end: *You need to let go of the past to welcome the future.*

It was a lesson that seemed particularly poignant as I realized I had reached the halfway point of my cross-country adventure—twenty-five states down, twenty-five to go! I was grasping the fact that I needed to leave behind what no longer fits to make space for new experiences and insights—so I can open doors I don't even know are there.

TRAVEL LOG

June 4, 2023

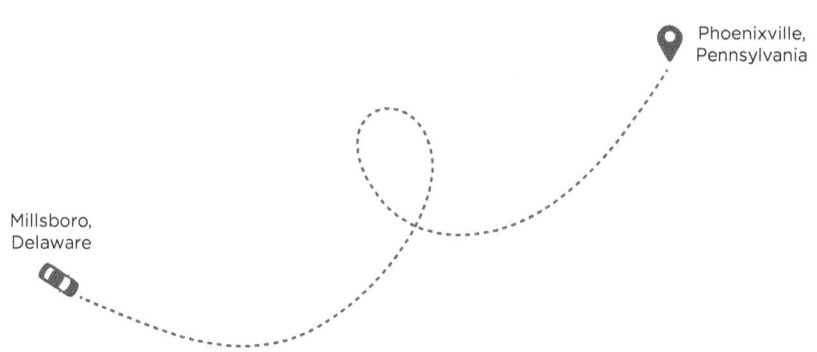

Deardra and me at Vintner's Table in Phoenixville, Pennsylvania

Table 26

Wine and Cheese at Vintner's Table Phoenixville, Pennsylvania

Deardra
Sunday, June 4, 2023—1:00 PM EDT

Deardra is fifty-three years old, and married for thirteen years with two school-aged daughters. She was born and raised in Seattle and moved to Pennsylvania about a decade ago, after attending college in the South and residing for several years in Virginia. She works as an IT Specialist.

Deardra, or "Dee Dee" as her friends affectionately call her, has always been more than just a friend to me; she's a piece of my childhood, a fragment of my heart. Picture it: two kids, each the sole offspring in their home, growing up side by side. Dee Dee's house was always alive with extended family, including an uncle who was just about our age; *my* world was quieter, framed by my adoptive parents and the pitter-patter of our miniature dachshund's feet.

Dee Dee's roots trace back to Louisiana, her grandparents bearing the heavy legacy of surviving segregation as Black Southerners. My family history, on the other hand, is woven with the stories of my Japanese American parents and their resilience through the hardships of World War II. As children, these profound histories were just tales of the past that our families shared—their true depth and sacrifice only fully sinking in as we grew older.

Dee Dee and I were raised in the 98118, a corner of Seattle known for its dazzling cultural mosaic, perhaps one of the most diverse ZIP codes in the nation back then. Our neighborhood was a vibrant mixture of Black, Brown, and a few White families. From the outside it was viewed as the humble side of town; but to us, it was a neighborhood filled with endless adventures. In a bittersweet reflection, Dee Dee and I realized that we stood out as the only ones from our childhood gang to have stepped into the halls of a university. Many from our circle weren't so lucky, their potential clipped short by life's hardships.

Time and life nudged Dee Dee and me onto different paths. Inseparable playmates in our earliest years, our friendship was eventually reduced to sporadic but cherished meetups. Yet, with every chance encounter—perhaps a fleeting moment on the sidewalk while getting into our cars to drive off to our separate high schools—it was like no time had passed at all. It struck me, as we spent our rare day together in Phoenixville, that despite how close we were as little girls, we had probably spent less than twenty-four hours together total since our grade-school years.

As we wandered through our memories, sharing a gorgeous charcuterie and cheese board while sipping wine made in Pennsylvania, we marveled at the rich cultural tapestry of our upbringing. I remember clearly the warmth of Dee Dee's family kitchen, where the scents of soul food filled the air. And I recall the laughter in my childhood living room, where the aromas of Japanese cooking drifted through. It was in this sandbox of our childhood that our attitude of ease and love for people from all backgrounds was nurtured.

As we hugged goodbye, Dee Dee left me with words that echoed in my soul: "You are not just my friend; you are my sister." In those few words, she had captured the essence of our bond, a connection deep-seated in our shared experience of childhood. And it was then that I realized: For all these years, we've each carried a piece of one another within us.

March 23, **2024**

Dear Diary,

As I continue editing my manuscript, revisiting all the places I've been, one of the things that I've been thinking about—in addition to all the meals I shared with the women I met—is how I'd always tried to squeeze in a visit to a Civil Rights Museum whenever there was one nearby, if I had a moment to spare. It kind of threw me for a loop when I discovered that Seattle's busing program from the seventies, which kept going into the eighties, was nationally recognized as groundbreaking—a lone-wolf city's voluntary efforts to integrate schools racially.

Living in the less-well-off part of Seattle, where historic racial covenants had cornered Brown, Black, and Jewish families into a few select neighborhoods, I had a firsthand view of these dynamics. This was the reality of South Seattle. While the South and Central areas were known for being on the lower end of the economic spectrum, the North was a whole other world—with White, middle- to upper-class families.

Not too long ago, I got to catch up with Bill, an old friend from high school who came from one of those more well-to-do Seattle neighborhoods. He was part of the first bunch of kids who got bused over to South Seattle before it was something every kid had to do. Hearing about his experiences as one of the only White kids in his new school, and how he managed to make friends through sports, was really something. Even as a young kid in first grade, he could see the financial differences just by looking at the birthday gifts he received—from the usual toys and games to a stolen library book from a pal who couldn't afford anything else. And then, driving his friends through neighborhoods where he was the odd one out, after football practice in high school, really shifted his view on things; it affected how he relates to people now. It taught him empathy in a way nothing else could.

It's strange, but my travels across the states have opened my eyes in a similar way. I'm incredibly grateful to all the women in this project and to everyone I've met along the way. They've helped me see the world through their eyes and understand the beautifully complex nature of our human story.

Feeling humbled,

Shari

TRAVEL LOG

June 4, 2023

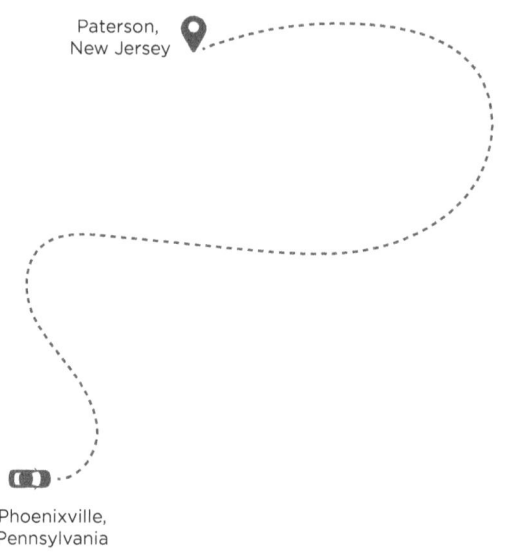

Talena and me at Hacienda in Paterson, New Jersey

Table 27

Dinner at Hacienda
Paterson, New Jersey

Talena
Sunday, June 4, 2023—6:00 PM EDT

Talena is fifty years old and a mom to four—three daughters and one son. She has been in a committed relationship for several years. She was born and raised in Paterson and returned to her home city eight years ago, after living in Washington State. She is a teacher, poet, and entrepreneur.

During this stretch of my adventure, I had the good fortune of spending time with Talena. In a playful confession, she told me she was hitting the big five-oh, something she had joked about being for a little while before it was actually true. I asked her, "How do you feel about getting older?" She answered with a big smile and a shrug, brushing off the serious labels other people often try to stick on us.

As someone who writes poetry and teaches, she knows her way around the power of words. She is acutely aware of how words can bring us together or push us apart.

My connection to Talena goes back to a quick hello at a dinner in Seattle almost ten years back. Our paths didn't cross again following that dinner so long ago, but thanks to the world of social media, we kept up with each other. When I was piecing together this project and found out that she had left Washington State, getting in touch with her felt like the right move. Her excited agreement to meet was like receiving a present.

Over dinner—which was chips, salsa, guacamole, and yummy Mexican cuisine—I could barely keep up with the pearls of wisdom Talena kept dropping on me. She's not just any poet; she's a shining light in her community as the Poet Laureate of Paterson, New Jersey! Talena is also a teacher, and the founder of the Paterson Poetry Festival. She is the brains behind a non-profit that's all about helping writers grow. Her words are weighty—filled with truth, wisdom, and the stuff of real life.

Talena's personal story is about bouncing back and pushing forward. She was born to teen-aged parents who were dealing with a lot. Her father struggled all his life with bouts of homelessness, battling addiction—but despite her family's troubles, Talena turned into a ray of hope and success in her family and community. When she moved back to Paterson after years on the West Coast, she got back in touch with her dad. He was without a home, so she made it a point to share meals and take time to talk with him, often finding him at a bus stop where he liked to hang out.

She told me about a funny incident. One time when her dad was at the bus stop, two ladies were handing out flyers that contained information on where he could go to get some help. He debated with them. He told the women that God would provide. And just moments later, while still in conversation with them, Talena unexpectedly showed up, with something to eat. Grinning from ear to ear, he announced to the ladies, "See? I told you! God provides."

Talena is a natural student and teacher. Her success in education shines brightly, as she's completed undergrad and graduate degrees and has almost completed her doctoral studies. Her message, especially meaningful when she talks to teachers, is all about seeing the potential in every student.

TABLE 27

I told her about a recent conversation I'd had with someone, in which I'd wanted to challenge and educate that person regarding their misguided stereotypes, but I'd chosen not to speak up. Talena shared a Buddhist principle: "When the student is ready, the teacher will come." She explained to me that that person simply wasn't ready; so it wasn't my place in that instance to be the teacher.

In an acceptance speech she gave after receiving an education award from the New Jersey Clean Communities Council—for starting a free book exchange program for young people in public parks—Talena remarked, "I am not supposed to be here, but I am," alluding to her humble beginnings.

Her words struck a chord with me. Reflecting on my own journey—from being an orphan found in a cardboard box, and then raised by parents who were interned during WWII—I realize that I too am not supposed to be here. Yet, here I am, an Asian American woman traveling across the USA, metaphorically flipping that cardboard box upside-down and turning it into a table—breaking bread with strangers, and discovering how connected we are to one another.

March 16, **2024**

Dear Diary,

Oh, covid! It finally caught me. And just when I had a date lined up with this man I'm absolutely crazy about. This would've been date number four—although he insists our first hangout was just a "meet and greet," not a real date.

I really do like him. We've got tons of mutual friends and our lives are stitched together with so many quirky coincidences. Our dating dance has been slow, partly because I told him—and all my potential dates—that I was only up for first dates this year. Second dates? Those were on hold until 2025. Seriously, that's what I told all of them—that if we clicked and we were both still single, then sure, we'd reconnect in 2025. My plan for going on just first dates this year was to figure out three things: 1) who's out there, 2) what traits I mesh with; and frankly, 3) if I'm even someone guys want to date.

But that plan flew out the window fast, especially after I met him.

So, here's hoping we can reschedule for next week—exactly two weeks since our last date. I'm trying not to get too attached to how things turn out, but I can't help wanting to give this a real shot. I've decided that I'll put a pause on dating anyone else for now.

And then there's Dana, my friend who comes up with the funniest nicknames. She called a guy I went out with (just before this man) "the pauper"—which makes this new guy feel a lot like "the prince" by comparison. Something about him just feels like what *home* is supposed to be: safe and warm.

Hopeless romantic,

Shari

TRAVEL LOG

June 5, 2023

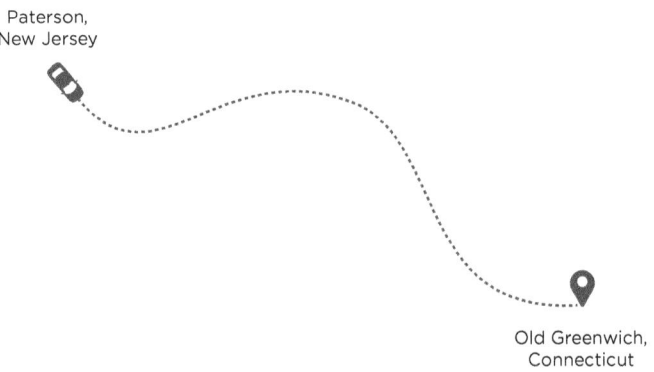

Kate and me at Alpen Pantry in Old Greenwich, Connecticut

Table 28

Sandwich Take-Out from Alpen Pantry Old Greenwich, Connecticut

Kate
Monday, June 5, 2023—11:00 AM EDT

Kate is fifty-four years old and mom to an adult daughter. She and her husband have been married for eleven years. She was born in Palo Alto, California and moved to Old Greenwich, Connecticut with her parents when she was just four years of age. After attending college in Boston, she returned to Greenwich to start a career and family. Kate is a seasoned marketing consultant. We were connected through a mutual friend.

Before today, Kate and I were just names to each other, linked by a friend we both very much appreciate. It's funny how you can just know you're about to bump into someone special. I'd heard about Greenwich, sure, but it was more like a storybook place than a real one to me. Stepping into Greenwich was like walking into a new world. Kate's roots run deep here, in the heart of Old Greenwich. It's where she grew up and where her family was established.

    Kate figured that the best way to show me who she is would be to show me around the sites that shaped her. So we kicked off at her place, then hit the road to a welcoming little sandwich spot run by brothers who know everyone in town. And talk about timing. Their mom was there, chatting up Kate like they were old pals. Walking out of there, Kate was telling me all about how Greenwich is more than just a place; it's a community—a web of stories and shared memories.

Next up was Tod's Point, a picture-postcard park by the beach. Of course, Kate is on a first-name basis with the guard at the gate. That beach is her haven, a place for quiet walks and smelling the sea air. We meandered around, past folks lost in books or soaking up the sun, with the New York City skyline beckoning us from a distance. It felt magical, like a secret pocket of peace. We found a picnic table where we could devour our sandwiches.

During our lunch, Kate opened up about dealing with her husband's grave illness. She knew that she would soon lose him—and she had to face that painful reality. Then she started talking about her friends from high school, a supportive band of brainy, witty souls who've somehow managed to keep the laughter going, even from miles apart. They catch up on Zoom, keeping the connection alive. And then there's Belinda, our mutual friend, bridging East to West with phone calls that double as walking tours. It's through these threads of friendship that Kate finds strength.

As I traveled on, my mind kept drifting back to my own circle of friends, the ones who have always been my anchors. It made me think about who's there for me and who needs me to be there for them.

My visit with Kate wasn't just about seeing Greenwich through her eyes; it was a reminder of how rich and vital our connections are. Friendships weave through our lives, bringing us closer no matter the distance. I was thankful for the day, for Kate, and for the vital lesson that cherishing our friendships will help us weather any storm.

TRAVEL LOG

June 17, 2023

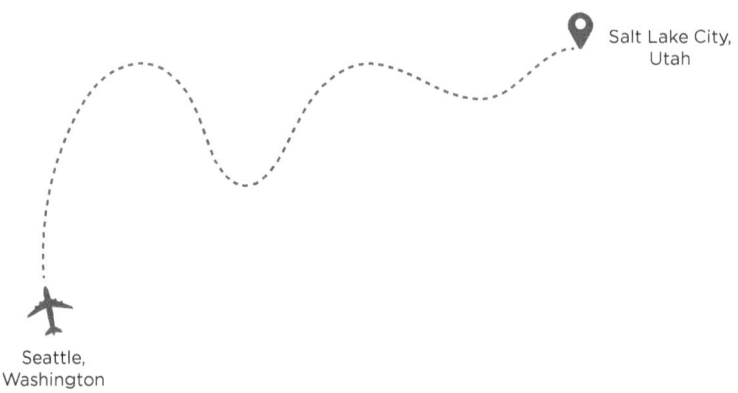

Talar and me at The Copper Onion in Salt Lake City, Utah

Table 29

Lunch at The Copper Onion
Salt Lake City, Utah

Talar
Saturday, June 17, 2023—12:30 PM MDT

Talar is a forty-eight-year-old Armenian American woman who has been married for twelve years. She has four kids—three who are her adult stepchildren, and one biological son. She was born to parents of Armenian heritage in Beirut, Lebanon, and grew up in Saudi Arabia until age twelve when her family immigrated to the United States. She has lived in Utah since 2009. Talar is a practicing attorney.

We were brought together through the serendipitous web of LinkedIn connections, courtesy of a fellow attorney we both knew virtually but had never met in person. In a peculiar twist of fate, not only were Talar and I complete strangers when our paths first crossed, but the kind-hearted connector who linked us remained a stranger as well.

Talar is the first and only person I've ever shared a meal with who was born in Beirut, Lebanon. Her early years were spent in Saudi Arabia, where her parents relocated when she was a child. It was during her time at an American school in Saudi Arabia that she took on the label of *Armenian American*, even though she had not yet become an American citizen nor set foot on American soil. When she was twelve years old, Talar's family moved to California—an incredibly huge cultural change for her during her formative years. She moved to Utah as an adult, after meeting her husband.

For this meeting I flew in from Seattle and flew back the same day. In our short time together, Talar and I discovered a striking array of commonalities: We're both immigrants, both attorneys, both authors with published works, both married to legal professionals, and both life coaches! Our shared interests were fun to talk about. However, what lingered in my thoughts since our parting was our profound discussion about the quest for community where we could find a sense of belonging.

As we delved into a discussion around our deliberate efforts to find community, the thought *Does this place feel like home?* crept into my mind. It was a question that has been my constant traveling companion. While engrossed in our conversation, I noticed Talar's gaze fixating on a family of five being seated at the adjacent table. A subtle smile graced her lips, revealing something I had initially missed: They were conversing in Armenian.

In an instinctive gesture, Talar leaned over and addressed the family in their native tongue. I witnessed a remarkable transformation in the family's demeanor, as surprise gave way to twinkling eyes. An immediate recognition and connection unfolded. As a mere observer, recently musing on the concept of finding one's place in the world, it was a heartwarming sight to see Talar's face light up while conversing with this family, also proficient in English—right here in Salt Lake City, Utah.

Watching this encounter evoked memories of my recent experience in South Dakota when I'd taken time out to visit Mount Rushmore. I spotted a man sporting a Washington State Cougar's T-shirt, and enthusiastically exclaimed, "Go Cougs!" to his delight. I playfully disclosed to him that, although I'm a University of Washington Husky, my father-in-law had been a professor at Washington State. His witty response—"At least one person in the family was smart!"—triggered knowing laughter. In this far-off place, our shared connection as fellow Washingtonians had forged an immediate sense of home.

My visit to Pennsylvania also came to mind, when I'd met with my childhood neighbor, Deardra, with whom I had played together daily until I was five. Despite the nearly fifty years that had elapsed, an immediate bond was rekindled through our shared childhood experiences of growing up on the same street.

All of these encounters were rooted in the ties that bind us—our cultural heritage, our place of residence, our childhood neighborhoods. This experience confirms my belief: If we can uncover our shared experiences, the buds of friendship will naturally blossom.

As we left the restaurant, Talar stopped to introduce me to the Armenian American family with a warm smile, saying, "This is my friend, Shari."

TRAVEL LOG

June 24, 2023

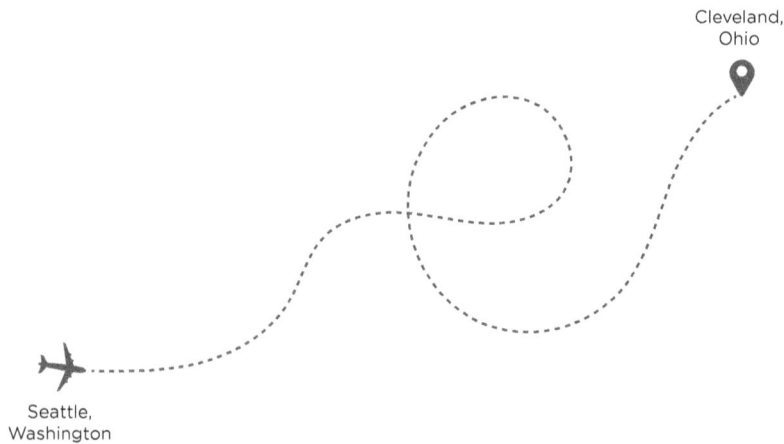

Farrah and me at Astoria Cafe & Market in Cleveland

June 24, **2023**

Dear Diary,

The day I landed in Cleveland, Ohio felt like stepping into one those news stories, the kind where you think you know what's going to happen but then—whoa, everything changes. There I was, in the shuttle from the airport to the car-rental place, and boom: My eyes caught something totally unexpected. Police cars and, get this, flags with symbols of White Supremacy. It was a parade of cars, a rally.

This was a punch in the gut, a real eye-opener that made my heart do somersaults.

Cleveland? Really? I had psyched myself up for maybe running into this sort of thing down South, where history's shadows linger. But every time I went there, people couldn't have been nicer, welcoming me with open arms. So, this—this was a curveball.

My hands started to shake a little as I drove, thoughts racing like I was the main character in a thriller, navigating a plot twist I never saw coming. Due to my terrible sense of direction and unfamiliarity with the streets, I ended up driving right *toward* the rally instead of away from it. In my mind, I pictured a news headline, the kind that makes your heart stop: *Asian woman accidentally crashes White Supremacy gathering.* That could have been me, in 64-point bold type. By the time I got to my hotel, my hands were trembling.

Later, I tried to make sense of it all by digging into some facts about Ohio, and what I found made my heart sink even more. Turns out, Ohio's got a pretty dark side when it comes to racism, topping charts for racist tweets in recent years. That realization just broke my heart.

This whole thing has made me think hard about my 50 States Project—sharing meals, hitting the road, talking to folks from every corner of life. It's clearer than ever how much we need to do this—to tear down walls and build bridges. And yeah, it's also thrown in my face that I'm not your average traveler. An Asian woman in her fifties, on a solo trek across the United States over the course of thirty-three weeks—dining with strangers? It's definitely not your everyday itinerary.

But after today, I need a moment. A deep breath. Maybe two. Tomorrow, I'll pick myself up, dust myself off, and keep going. Because that's what this journey is teaching me: how to find the courage to move forward, even when the road takes a sharp turn you never saw coming.

With a hopeful heart,

Shari

Table 30

Brunch at Astoria Cafe & Market
Cleveland, Ohio

Farrah
Sunday, June 25, 2023—10:30 AM EDT

Farrah is forty-six years old, married for twenty years. They have no children. Born and raised in Ohio, she works as a Project Manager.

Over a decade ago, Farrah moved to Seattle, Washington because of her husband's job opportunity—a decision that altered her life's path, if only for a short while. Their stay in Seattle was brief—a mere two years—but it was during this period that our paths crossed at a couple of big social gatherings. Little did I realize then that these sporadic meetings were the early roots of a lasting friendship.

When I decided to embark on this journey across the States, I immediately thought that this would be a great opportunity to reconnect with Farrah. I reached out and invited her to be part of my project, asking her to choose where we would meet. Her choice was a Mediterranean eatery and marketplace, a trendy spot offering awesomely curated food boards featuring gourmet meats and Mimosa flights. The "Bubbles Board"—a strikingly crafted charcuterie and cheese board—became the backdrop for our reconnection.

Upon my arrival, I began my familiar routine of setting up my video and photo equipment. This time, however, I was navigating a new lighting system, having absentmindedly left my usual equipment on a plane to Salt Lake City. Farrah's bright energy and adventurous spirit turned this challenge into the perfect kickoff to a morning filled with laughter.

As we sat together, surrounded by vibrant greenery and bathed in sunlight, our conversation unfolded naturally. Farrah knew more about me than I knew of her, because of my constant over-sharing on social media. This imbalance sparked a morning filled with discoveries.

Our talk meandered through memories of life experiences, from how we met our spouses, to our college years, and reminiscences of our childhoods. But it was Farrah's story of being an adoptee that resonated with me the most.

Farrah's journey, like mine, was one of self-discovery. Raised by her stepfather, whom she adored as her dad, she grew up not knowing her biological dad. This part of her life, a relationship with her biological dad, unfolded unexpectedly. Her reunion with her biological father's family came about not through active searching but through a chance volleyball game with her aunt. Unbeknownst to Farrah, she had been playing recreational volleyball with her biological aunt. Farrah's mom recognized this woman when she attended one of Farrah's games. This chance meeting led Farrah to meet her biological father and his family, giving her a deeper understanding of her own identity. She learned where certain traits and characteristics had come from—pieces of her own puzzle falling into place in a way she had never known before.

As our time together came to an end, our waitress commented on the strong connection she observed between us, mistaking us for long-time friends. It was a testament to our natural and easy bond.

I could not have anticipated that Farrah's story of reconnection with her biological family would be a precursor to another remarkable story I would hear later that day in Michigan.

TABLE 30

Reflecting on my initial discomfort when I first arrived in Cleveland, contrasted with the effortless and wonderful connection I made with Farrah, I am reminded that sheer enjoyment, beauty, and love exist everywhere—even in places where we initially fail to see them.

TRAVEL LOG

June 25, 2023

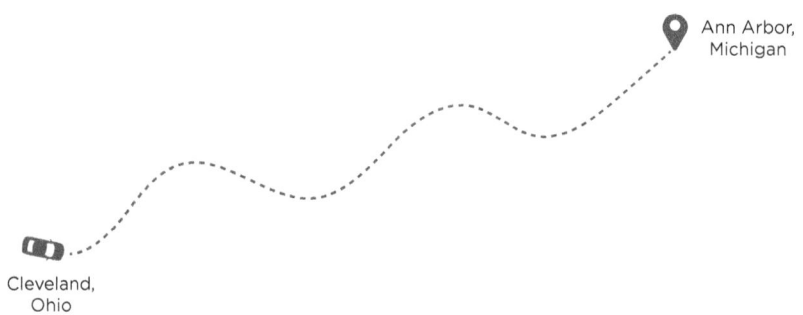

Angela and Me at Seoul Garden

Table 31

Dinner at Seoul Garden
Ann Arbor, Michigan

Angela
Sunday, June 25, 2023—6:00 PM EDT

Angela is a forty-eight-year-old Korean American. She is a single mother to an adult son. Born in Busan, South Korea, she was adopted at six months of age, and raised in Michigan by a White family with an older sister who was her adoptive parents' biological daughter. Angela works as a hospice nurse.

In 2013, in the sprawling universe of Facebook, Angela and I somehow found each other. I can't for the life of me remember who friended whom. My motto then was *the more the merrier*, especially if anyone was part of the Korean adoptee groups I was exploring. Time passed, and my Facebook friends list eventually got a major trim, down to just the folks I actually knew. But then, as luck would have it, when I was searching for someone from Michigan, Angela's name popped right up. We were still Facebook friends! We had never messaged, called, or emailed, yet finding her felt like uncovering a hidden gem. I didn't hesitate to ask her to join my 50 States Project.

Growing up on the West Coast in proximity to a large South Korean immigrant community, you'd think I'd have met other Korean adoptees all the time. But no, Angela was *the first one!* She was amazed by that. My folks, Asian Americans who adopted me when international adoption was just starting to be a thing in the United States, didn't really chase down those connections. Maybe they didn't see the need since we weren't an interracial family—despite the vast differences between their Japanese American culture and my Korean culture. Michigan, Angela's place, was a whole different world—with active agencies and a considerable community of Korean adoptees.

We decided that it would be fun to share a Korean meal together, so Angela found the perfect Korean BBQ place. Our conversation focused a lot on adoption. There's a definite pull, whenever I meet another adopted person, to dig into their adoption story. Angela's—and others, like Mai Lara's from New York—felt both different and familiar. Both of them were Asian adoptees growing up in a White family, a contrast to my own upbringing.

Hearing about Angela's trips to South Korea—especially one that changed everything for her, was incredibly interesting. Several years ago, she had used DNA testing to trace her roots, which led her to a biological relative in the States, who then connected her to her biological father's family. Angela said that meeting her dad and half-brothers in South Korea was like looking into a mirror—seeing for herself their notable family resemblances.

Thinking over Angela's story, her involvement in the Korean adoptee community, and how she's embraced Korean culture and language, has made me wonder what the effect would be on me if *I* were to make the effort to become more connected to my birthplace and to other Korean adoptees. I can't remember now if I asked Angela which felt more like home to her—South Korea or Michigan. That will be a question for the next time we meet.

March 3, 2024

Dear Diary,

I had the best time yesterday celebrating with my son, Zach, at Disneyland and California Adventure—celebrating his twenty-second birthday. He sent me the most heartwarming text afterwards saying the day was perfect, and his best birthday ever.

My heart is full.

With so much love,

Shari

TRAVEL LOG

July 7, 2023

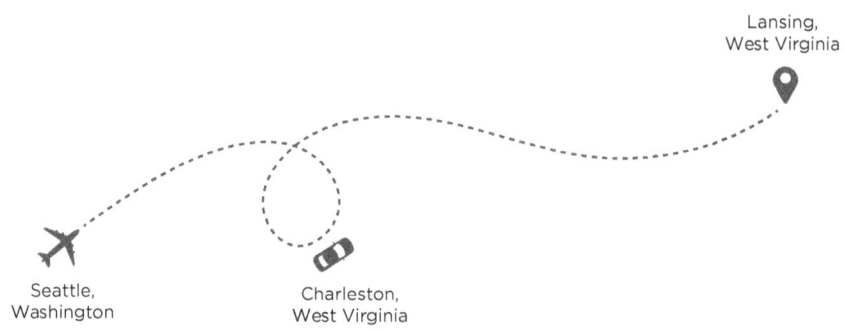

Twanna and me at Smokey's on the Gorge in Lansing, West Virginia

Table 32

Dinner at Smokey's on the Gorge Lansing, West Virginia

Twanna
Saturday, July 8, 2023—5:00 PM EDT

Twanna is forty-two years old and engaged to be married. She has two daughters—one who is in her teens and the other an adult. She was born and raised in West Virginia, and she works as an advocate for victims and clients.

It was quite a trip, starting from Seattle and ending up in Charleston, West Virginia. I'd had a lengthy layover in Atlanta with a one-hour drive to my destination: a charmingly furnished glamping tent in the quaint town of Hico, just a stone's throw away from Lansing, West Virginia. By the time I arrived and settled in, it was almost midnight, but I decided to set my alarm for an early morning hike.

When the alarm jolted me awake, I was greeted by the most beautiful sunny day—the perfect backdrop for my hike. My guide for the day was Maureen, a Korean American woman who had relocated from Washington, DC to West Virginia during the pandemic. We shared a laugh over the odds of finding another Korean American in West Virginia.

As we trekked through the scenic landscape, I took in the beauty of the surroundings—the majestic tree-covered mountains, the wild flora, and the meandering river—all of which reminded me of the geography back home in Washington State. Even the moss adorning the tree trunks and rocks had a similar appearance. As it turns out, West Virginia and Washington share the same official state flower, the rhododendron. My introduction to West Virginia had been nothing short of spectacular. I couldn't wait to meet Twanna later that day.

As fate would have it, Twanna suggested we meet at a restaurant located at the very spot where I had embarked on my morning hike: New River Gorge in Lansing. It was the ideal setting for our warm conversation and shared meal, which included West Virginia pepperoni rolls (think pigs-in-a-blanket—that's how I described them). We greeted each other with hugs and delved straight into our chat. Dana, my girlfriend in Seattle, had connected me with Twanna; all she knew about her was that she hailed from the small West Virginia town of Pineville. Dana had last seen Twanna over thirty-five years ago! She was eager to learn what had led Twanna from Pineville to where she is now.

I learned that Twanna's move had been prompted by tragedy: a devastating flood in 2001 that obliterated Pineville and left her family with nothing. After meeting Twanna, I read reports on the flood at the time. It is hard to fathom living through such utter devastation, which had unfolded in a matter of hours without any warning. Roads were washed away, and at least eleven state bridges were destroyed. The aftermath had forced Twanna and her family into homelessness, living in a motel for months until they could rebuild their lives.

What struck me during our conversation was Twanna's ability to narrate these life-altering events without letting them define her. Whether her stories were tragic or triumphant, they were just part of her life's narrative, with neither victim nor hero status attached. The experiences were like ingredients or spices—adding flavor, but not overpowering the essence of who she is.

TABLE 32

Twanna approached her racial identity in a similar manner. Growing up as the only Black family in her small town—and one of just a handful of Black students in her high school—appears very challenging to me, but she seemed almost dismissive of it. She explained that it wasn't a major issue for her because she has always been proud of her identity and of her family of origin. Her mom, whom I had the pleasure of meeting, raised Twanna with the belief that true value comes from within. She taught Twanna the vital importance of self-awareness over external appearances.

Our time together passed in a flash. Just as it had been for Twanna growing up—and still is today—our different racial backgrounds and life experiences didn't matter in the slightest. We left each other's company feeling like sisters, with hopes of reuniting in the future.

As a final note, I asked Twanna about her thoughts on aging. She responded with the same enthusiasm and positivity that had permeated our entire meal. "I'm excited about it. Because my family ages beautifully," she declared.

I feel privileged to call Twanna a friend, someone I now consider family. I look forward to aging beautifully right alongside Twanna—and with all the women who have become my friends across the USA.

March 25, **2024**

Dear Diary,

Imagine this: Last night felt like I was living inside the best romance novel! Seriously, it was the best date of my life. We've been out three times before, but this guy, he just keeps surprising me in the best ways possible. Whenever I'm with him, it's like time just speeds up, flying by without a care.

After he cooked an absolutely amazing dinner (yeah, he cooks!), he decided to ramp up the evening's entertainment with a karaoke session right in his living room. And guess what? The first song we ended up singing was my secret favorite, though I hadn't mentioned it to him. Somehow, it was like he just knew. It was that hit *Shallow*, by Lady Gaga and Bradley Cooper, the one that always manages to pull at my heartstrings.

Standing there, microphones in hand, we transformed his living room into our own little concert. It was one of those moments where you feel completely free and happy.

And here's a little tidbit: The song we sang is the same one that Hannah, from California, had on her list for me to learn in her music studio. I never got around to it back then because we were focusing on something simpler. But I think she'd be over the moon to know I finally sang it—and with someone who's starting to feel a lot like home.

Best date ever!

Giddy,

Shari

TRAVEL LOG

July 14, 2023

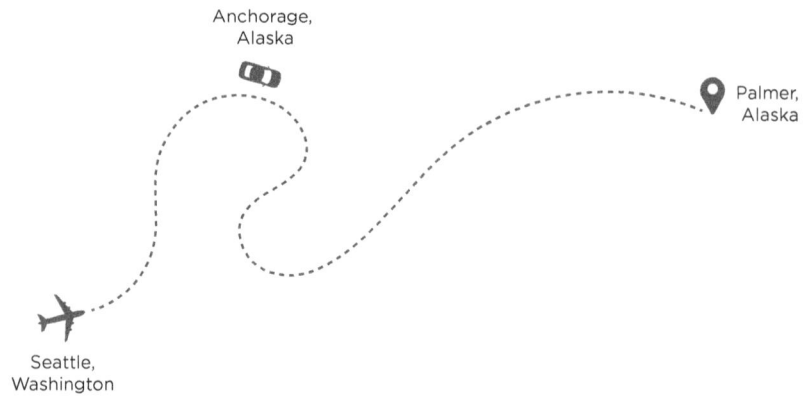

Noel and me at Turkey Red in Palmer, Alaska

Table 33

Brunch at Turkey Red
Palmer, Alaska

Noel
Saturday, July 15, 2023—11:00 AM Alaska Daylight Time

Noel is a fifty-nine-year-old woman, divorced, with two teen-aged children. She was born in Texas and has lived most of her life in Alaska. Noel has worked in Social Services, and she is also a talented artist.

In the swirl of this phenomenal journey, I crossed paths with Noel. She's teetering at the edge of her sixties—a decade she's stepping into with grace. Every time I meet women who are dancing into their sixties, it's like peering through a window into what's waiting for me just around the corner. And Noel is a guiding star in that night sky—reminding me of Talena back in New Jersey, with her completely unbothered attitude towards aging.

To Noel, age is just a number; it doesn't get to tell her what she can or can't do. Sure, she's realistic about the things that change with time—like debating the value of going back to school at this point in her life—but she doesn't let the number on her birthday cake dictate her capacity to dream or achieve.

It was my first time visiting Alaska—and Palmer didn't disappoint. About an hour's drive from Anchorage, the small town of Palmer has an Old Wild West charm, with friendly people. I even took a line-dancing class, which was a blast!

Noel suggested we meet at a charming restaurant which prided itself on sourcing over seventy percent of its ingredients locally. While we were there, she shared the fascinating history of Palmer with me. In 1935, under President Franklin Roosevelt's New Deal, the Federal Emergency Relief Administration established the Matanuska Valley Colony. From the drought-ridden Midwest, over 200 families from Minnesota, Wisconsin, and Michigan made the long journey by train and ship to this new frontier. That first Alaskan Summer, they lived in a tent city. Each family drew lots for forty-acre tracts, embarking on a farming adventure in this beautiful, wild land.

Spending time with Noel unfolded like a storybook adventure. She lives life spectacularly free from the *shoulds* and *musts* that beliefs about aging try to impose upon us. She told me that her faith is a private affair—something personal and direct—much like the conversations I've found myself having with God on this trip.

Delving into Noel's past was just as fascinating as her present. Her early life started with her parents in Oregon, with moves through a childhood marked by change, until they settled in Alaska—where the backdrop of her younger years feels straight out of a frontier tale. Her mother, who traded high school for early marriage and found her independence behind a bar after her divorce, instilled in Noel and her sister a strong sense of community and resilience.

Reviewing Noel's social media accounts before our brunch, I learned that she graduated from Syracuse University. I wondered, after hearing about her upbringing, how a daughter of a single mom—a bartender who never even finished high school—charted her course to such a prestigious place. Noel told me that she credits hard work, a solo cross-country drive with nothing but her cat for company, and an unwavering faith in the kindness of strangers and the guidance of a Higher Power.

Noel's take on friendship is as unique as she is. She described her circle as "Fireweed Friends"—a nod to the pink-petaled, sturdy and vibrant plant that thrives in Alaska: Tough, low-maintenance, and lovely, they stand by her through thick and thin.

With all this traveling across our country, I was starting to notice a transformation within myself. Reflecting on my many encounters, the wisdom Noel shared from her father stood out: "There's a difference between running *away* and running *to*."

As I left the pioneering spirit of Alaska, I realized I was actually filled with excitement for the unknown. This ongoing journey, with all its revelations, is not an escape from; it's a pursuit toward something extraordinary.

February 13, **2024**

Dear Diary,

Just a quick note: I want to remember Noel's words, from our meetup in Alaska, as I ponder so many things—moving homes, looking at career opportunities, and some day falling in love again—I want to make sure that with all that I am doing, I am *running to* and not *running from*.

Thanks Noel.

Best,

Shari

TRAVEL LOG

July 19, 2023

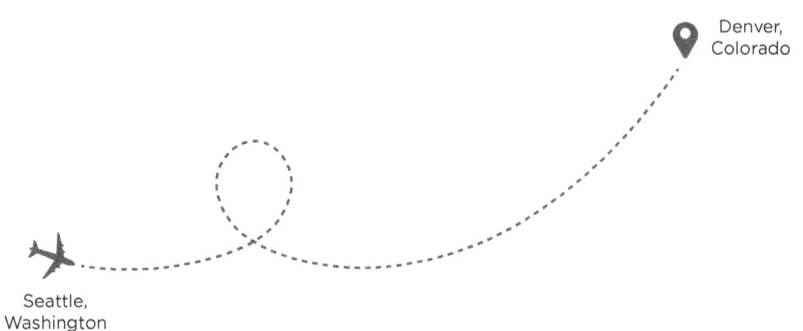

Connie and me at True Food Kitchen, Cherry Creek North, Denver, Colorado

Table 34

Dinner at True Food Kitchen, Cherry Creek North Denver, Colorado

Connie
Friday, July 21, 2023—5:00 PM MDT

Connie and I are the same age, fifty-three. She was born in Jackson, Mississippi. While she has lived in several different states, she says that Colorado, where she has lived for several years, feels the most like home. She is married, and mom to an adult daughter. She is a small business owner.

Connie and I had crossed paths once before, back in 2020, during a birthday brunch I hosted at my home. She was visiting Washington State from Colorado, invited as a guest by one of our mutual friends. Given the short duration of the two-hour brunch, with a group of women gathered around my ten-person dining room table, Connie and I didn't have any time to get to know one another. When I decided to embark on my 50 States Project, she was the first person who came to mind located in Colorado, and I was thrilled when she eagerly agreed to participate.

Our time together in Denver's Cherry Creek area can only be described as pure joy. We felt like kindred spirits, each of us living our life as an open book. This became evident as we shared our life stories. Going over the highs and lows, and everything in between, we found ourselves laughing heartily. The happiness stemmed from the effortlessness of our instant connection.

Interestingly, the day before I met up with Connie, I'd spent the afternoon with my friend Melissa, who happens to be my former college freshman-year roommate. Meeting Connie felt just as familiar, even though we didn't share the same college memories as Melissa and I did.

Connie and I didn't hold back in our conversation. I even told her about my body insecurities, stemming from the physical scars that crisscross my body—from hip replacements to breast cancer scars. As I shared my marriage woes with Connie, I also said that I couldn't help but wonder that if I did go through with a divorce, how I would navigate dating and explaining my appearance to potential partners. Connie, without hesitation, responded, "If you meet the right person, you will never have to explain yourself." Her words struck a chord with me. And, unbeknownst to her, her words were giving me the strength to face why I'd stayed in my marriage. I saw that it was not just my financial fears but also, in great part, the fear that the scars my body carries will prevent me from finding love.

I loved that there was no awkwardness between us; we felt like old friends from the moment we met. We even indulged in an old-fashioned photo booth session in my hotel lobby, like old high-school friends.

As I drove to Wyoming the next morning, I felt a tug on my heartstrings. I found myself missing Connie's infectious energy and wishing we'd had more time. I was already looking forward to the next time we could get together.

TRAVEL LOG

July 22, 2023

Barb and me at FireRock Steakhouse

Table 35

Dinner at FireRock Steakhouse
Casper, Wyoming

Barb
Saturday, July 22, 2023—6:00 PM MDT

Barb is sixty-three years old, married with no children. She was born in Montana, resided in Casper, Wyoming for a few years as a child, and moved back as an adult. While she has lived and traveled to many places both in country and internationally, Casper, Wyoming is the place that feels like home for her. She is an airline pilot.

Today, I found myself weaving through the vast, open landscape of Wyoming, a far cry from the urban sprawl of Denver. It was my first-ever visit to the state. Its rugged, untamed beauty immediately struck me, evoking memories of my awe-inspiring trip to Uluru (Ayers Rock) in Australia. Wyoming's sprawling rock formations and wide-open skies whispered tales of the Wild West.

    The highlight of my day, however, was meeting Barb. Our connection was serendipitous, as we were brought together by her cousin Belinda, whom I knew from my kids' elementary school days. (Belinda was also the bridge to my meeting with Kate in Connecticut, making this encounter feel all the more predestined.)

Barb, initially uncertain about our meeting, had agreed to it out of trust in her cousin. I felt a deep sense of appreciation for her willingness to step into the unknown and share her evening with me. The weather was nice enough that we were able to sit outside. Our dinner unfolded into hours of effortless conversation, proving the power of new connections.

Barb is the epitome of adventure. Her life has been a series of bold choices, which I greatly admire. Her resume—as a commercial airline pilot, scuba diver, and motorcycle enthusiast—stands in stark contrast to my own seemingly less-daring pursuits. Our differences became a source of laughter, especially when we touched on the topic of public speaking—a fear of Barb's that I don't share. Her emphatic *Oh, nooooo!* to my raising the idea of her teaching aeronautics in a classroom only deepened my appreciation for the diversity of human experience.

Our conversation lingered on Barb's trailblazing career as a commercial airline pilot—a field in which you don't see very many women. Barb's journey to the skies was as unique as she is. It all started with a nudge from a community college counselor, and took off with her very first flight! She fell in love with flying and quickly realized that the only way she could afford to fly as often as she wanted was to make a career out of it.

That evening, we skipped the wine with our dinner because Barb was scheduled to fly within the next forty-eight hours. What I love about Barb's vocational choice is that it's not just that she became a pilot; it's a testament to following your passion, no matter the odds against you.

"Find something you love, and then figure out how to make a career out of it," Barb advised. This sentiment, which perfectly captures Barb's own path, resonated deeply with me. Her dedication to her passion, despite the challenges, is a powerful reminder of the joy and fulfillment that come from following your heart.

As our dinner conversation shifted to the topic of retirement—something I hadn't discussed with anyone else in this project—Barb shared her mixed feelings about approaching sixty-five, the mandatory retirement age for

TABLE 35

commercial airline pilots. Her talk about missing the camaraderie with her male colleagues struck a chord. It reminded me of my own departure from the practice of law, and how I missed the male energy and easy conversations that I was able to have simply by walking down the hallway into a co-worker's office—male connections and friendships that I haven't been able to replicate as a stay-at-home mom or as a solo business owner.

Parting from Barb, I couldn't help but remark on how quickly the time had flown, to which she quipped, "That's what happens when you meet with a pilot." Her witty and light response perfectly encapsulated the spirit of our meeting.

TRAVEL LOG

July 28, 2023

Lauren and me at Café Bossa Nova in Little Rock, Arkansas

Table 36

Lunch at Café Bossa Nova
Little Rock, Arkansas

Lauren
Saturday, July 29, 2023—11:00 AM CDT

Lauren is thirty-seven years old, married with three children. She was born and raised in Arkansas, moving out of the Little Rock area to attend college and law school in Fayetteville, and then moving back to Little Rock to start her family and career. Her husband also has deep roots in Arkansas. Lauren is a practicing attorney.

When Lauren and I first crossed paths, it felt like the stars had aligned just right—a sentiment I owe to my friend Jiawen. She's the link between us, through her husband's family. It's amazing, the way life pieces itself together: me, adopted from South Korea; Jiawen, a former exchange student from China who, after college, chose the United States as her home; and her husband, who journeyed from Arkansas to Seattle, where their lives merged.

All these twists of fate led me to sitting across from Lauren in a cozy restaurant in Little Rock, feeling the warmth of the owners—a family who made their way here from Brazil.

This was my second trip to Arkansas. The first one had been just a year prior—to adopt our Chocolate Labrador out of Siloam Springs, Arkansas—and just like the first time, I experienced nothing but exceptional Southern hospitality during this visit.

Lauren's the second lawyer I've met on my travels. There's a whisper of anticipation for the few other attorneys I will be meeting in the remaining states. Having left the law profession behind to focus on my family, these encounters with women attorneys are like finding a piece of home in an unexpected place—that instant, comforting connection you feel with someone from back in the day.

The restaurant, a favorite of Lauren and her husband, serves Brazilian food that's extra delicious—providing a comfortable atmosphere of home cooking. As Lauren shared her career plans and talked about her kids, I saw reflections of my younger self. I vividly remembered the times I tried to fit my life around my career—a jigsaw puzzle I wished I'd solved sooner. Lauren, though, seemed to be ahead of the curve, capably balancing her career with her roles in the community, her church, and her family—all with a grace I very much admire.

Sitting across from Lauren, I realized how every woman I meet mirrors some part of me. Lauren took me straight back to my own days at thirty-seven years old. As I reflected on a part of me I had not taken the time to think about until now, it made me proud of who I once was. I was managing the complexities of work, young children, a marriage, and friends back then—at what now seems to me to be a very young age.

March 4, 2024

Today's meditation mantra: *I love and accept all of me. I am at home within myself.*

TRAVEL LOG

August 3, 2023

Rhonda and me at her home in Great Falls, Montana

Table 37

Dinner at Rhonda's Home
Great Falls, Montana

Rhonda
Thursday, August 3, 2023—5:00 PM MDT

Rhonda is sixty-six years old. She is married with two adult children. She was born in Southern California, raised her family in Washington State, and moved to Great Falls, Montana roughly thirteen years ago—the place she now calls home. She is a fine arts photographer.

It feels like only yesterday that Rhonda and I first crossed paths. In her cozy little studio, she captured the kind of laughter from my two-year-old daughter that you wish you could bottle up and keep forever. Flash forward two years later, and Rhonda was taking pictures of our family again, this time with my son in the frame. Nineteen years have zipped by since then, and through the magic of social media, I discovered Rhonda had packed up her life in Washington State for the wide-open spaces of Montana—a state I'd never set foot in until today.

Rhonda was all in for a reunion and even invited me over to her place in Great Falls. Driving from the airport to my hotel, and then to Rhonda's, I immediately witnessed why Montana's "Big Sky Country" moniker made perfect sense. I couldn't help but wonder about the rest of Montana, especially since friends had mentioned that as lovely as Great Falls is, the rest of the state takes your breath away even more. But standing at the end of Rhonda's driveway, looking out at the vast, untouched panorama of nature, I found it hard to believe anything could be more stunning.

Rhonda's home reflected her artist's soul, just like Anna's in Arizona and Toni's in South Dakota. Every corner, every piece, told a part of her story—each element a testament to the heart of an artist—infusing life into every space she touches. Rhonda's art hung perfectly on her walls, reminding me of the pull I always feel toward the world of creativity—where words are my paint.

On the drive to the airport at the start of this trip, my driver Andrei told me about his father—a would-be artist in Belarus, whose spirit was beaten down by his surroundings, because he was unable to create and express himself the way his soul yearned. This tragic story contrasted sharply with Rhonda's fearless pursuit of her creative passions. It was an obvious reminder of the many freedoms we often take for granted here in America. My love for this spirited land we call home keeps growing deeper through my travels.

Rhonda moved to Montana after meeting her husband, embracing new beginnings in Great Falls at the age of fifty-three. She's living proof that it's never too late to find where you belong.

More than once my thought wandered back to the calm drive up to her home, the quiet peace that settles over you in Montana—the way the sunset paints everything gold. I remembered Rhonda's response when I texted her that my flight had been delayed, and I'd been rushing. She texted back: *You've done enough rushing.*

In her words, and in the serenity of her Montana home, I found a gentle reminder of life's pace—not measured in minutes or miles, but in memorable moments that take your breath away. Just like Montana's endless sky.

March 4, 2024

Dear Diary,

Today, as I prepped our family home for its next chapter, inviting painters to permeate the walls with fresh hope for someone else's new memories, a wave of unexpected emotion enveloped me. Amidst the flurry of organizing my manuscript and pouring my soul into it, a profound epiphany emerged—one that almost brought me to tears.

Not from sadness, but from a deep, soul-stirring awareness. For the first time, I truly grasped the essence of my journey through all 50 states.

Since the moment I was orphaned, my heart has been on a quest—a pursuit not fully understood until today—for a place that whispers, "You're home." This longing, this search for belonging, has quietly shaped my every step, my every decision.

Now, as I polish the final words of my story, a sense of closure is enveloping me, mingled with a burgeoning hope. I'm beginning to believe that, perhaps, I've finally found what my heart has been seeking. In the face of losing my physical house—a place I've called home for many years—I've come to a profound realization: It was necessary to release this space to discover what *home* truly means.

A home isn't just walls and a roof; it's where love resides, where the heart feels safe and cherished.

My 50 States Project has become a journey of the heart—unveiling, state by state, the true essence of *home*. Home is not just a place, but a feeling—a sanctuary where one is fully seen, and fully loved.

The road ahead is uncertain, yet for the first time, my heart is full of anticipation. I'm ready to build a life rooted in love, to fall deeply into the embrace of a community that feels like family. This journey has led me to extraordinary encounters and locales, granting me a sense of belonging and acceptance that transcends anything I could have imagined. Through the eyes of the remarkable women I've met, I've discovered the true meaning of safety. Of home.

With all my heart,

Shari

TRAVEL LOG

August 5, 2023

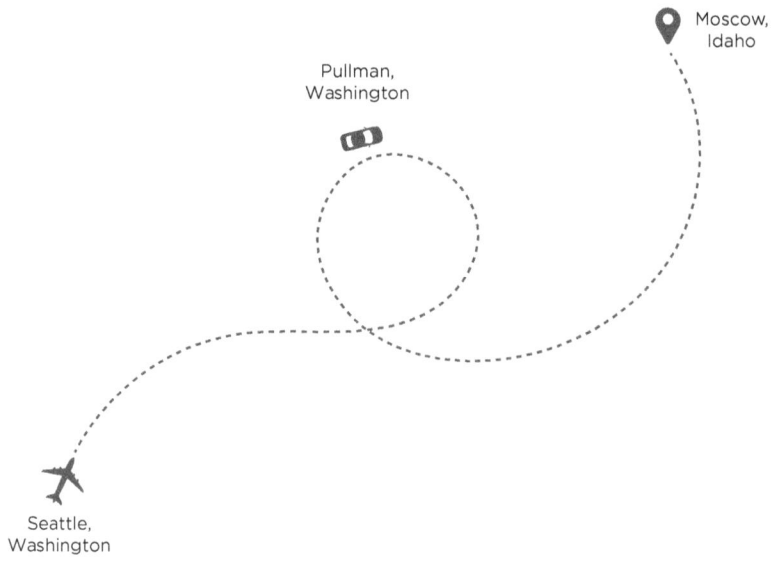

Dana and me at One World Café in Moscow, Idaho

Table 38

Drinks at One World Café and Dinner at Lodgepole
Moscow, Idaho

Dana
Saturday, August 5, 2023—4:00 PM PST

Dana is fifty-nine years old, married with no children. She is a director in higher education, working with international students and related programs.

Over a decade ago, I met Dana serendipitously: Her husband was my physical therapist, guiding me through the tricky recovery from hip surgery. I was only thirty-seven years old, suddenly dealing with a diagnosis of hip dysplasia, which left me with two artificial hips. Tonight, for the first time, Dana and I sat down to really get to know each other. The setting was perfect—the vibrant college town of Moscow, Idaho.

We started out with a glass of wine at One World Café, diving into a conversation that felt more like a baring of our souls than a casual meetup. Later, we joined Dana's husband for dinner at Lodgepole North American Kitchen, a fabulous restaurant where we enjoyed hearty American fare under sunny skies.

Dana shared that when she turned forty, nearly two decades ago, she experienced a profound internal shift—an epiphany that told her she was destined to do something impactful. She decided to channel her energy into supporting college students. She currently works with international students, guiding them through the complexities of adjusting to life in the United States. From their initial hopeful inquiries to navigating the intricacies of the visa process and cultural acclimatization, Dana is a steadfast advocate for equity and inclusion. Her commitment ensures that these students receive the same opportunities she had—leveling the playing field for those who may have started out having to deal with challenging circumstances.

As we shared our individual life experiences over dinner, nestled amidst the quaint bookstores and coffee shops that define the college-town aesthetic, I could sense Dana's strong commitment to justice and fairness for all. I asked Dana if her passion for justice was inherited from her family. Interestingly, she shared that her commitment to fairness and integrity was more a personal crusade than a family legacy. Dana has always been guided by a strong internal moral compass. Discussing her commitment to raising others up, I couldn't help but feel inspired by her tenacity.

Leaving the restaurant, the crisp evening air of Moscow was alive with the energy of the young minds around us. As I reflected on the great impact Dana is making in the world, it ignited a desire within me to discover how I, too, can contribute to making a positive and lasting impact on future generations.

The magic of this college town, where every street and corner hummed with possibilities, filled me with excitement about where my journey might lead to next. I prayed that I will be able to live in a way that positively impacts the world, just as Dana is doing—one student at a time.

After all, we are all each other's teachers—and students.

August 5, **2023**

Dear Diary,

My heart is heavy with a pain that's hard to articulate. When I arrived at the house, after leaving Dana and catching a late flight home, I walked in to find that my husband was not there. And he had left a mess, which led me to believe that he had been drinking. He had uncharacteristically forgotten his mobile phone at the house, which was sitting on his desk. I picked up his phone, and surprisingly it was open to messages he'd sent to other women—in particular, a woman he went to high school with, as well as a woman who was a former client.

I'm reeling, feeling lost in the life I thought I knew.

Today, I stumbled upon a quote that feels like a sign: "Addiction is surrendering everything for one thing. Recovery is forsaking one thing for everything." It resonates deeply in my soul, a beacon in the darkness of my confusion.

I'm allowing myself twenty-four hours to be sad.

With a shattered spirit,

Shari

August 6, **2023**

Dear Diary,

The twenty-four-hour mark has come and gone. It's clear—time's up. But the heart is not done. Healing, I'm learning, doesn't punch the clock.

My favorite quote keeps looping over and over in my thoughts: "If today were the last day of your life, would you be doing what you are doing now?" My answer is a loud, reverberating *No!* Neither sorrow nor anger deserves a starring role in my day.

Today felt like I was in a scene from someone else's life—one I never thought I'd be a part of: I started drafting separation paperwork and spoke with a friend who is a divorce attorney so I could understand the lay of the land that was before me.

In a moment of unfiltered truth, I stood before the mirror, bare. I took in every scar, every line—a silent testament to all the surgeries I've endured, the most defining being from my double mastectomy. It was a face-to-face with myself—a version I don't think I've truly seen until now.

But there's a sense of grounding taking hold. I found a way to see past the scars, to actually see *the real me*. Connie's wisdom from Colorado rings true: *When the right person comes along, my scars won't require an explanation.*

I feel like I'm living in a haze.

Embracing the journey even through the tears,

Shari

TRAVEL LOG

August 9, 2023

Judy and me at Apple Villa Pancake House in South Barrington, Illinois

Table 39

Lunch at Apple Villa Pancake House
South Barrington, Illinois

Judy
Thursday, August 10, 2023—11:30 AM CDT

Judy has been married for thirty-eight years. She was born in Iowa and moved to Illinois for work following college, where she met her husband and raised their children, who are now adults. At sixty-three, she continues to maintain the family home in Illinois, but also for the last seven years she has spent the majority of her time with her husband and son in St. Croix, one of the U.S. Virgin Islands in the Caribbean. She says she has found community there; it very much feels like home. She is a retired business owner and dog trainer.

Last year, when I started looking for women to connect with, I hit a roadblock at Illinois. So, I cast my net wider, tapping into an old online board from a media training group to which I'd once belonged. That's how I got connected to Judy, through a woman I don't even really know. I wasn't sure what their relationship was like, but as it turns out, they were as close as can be. I had never traveled to South Barrington and was pleasantly surprised to learn it was a suburb of the vibrant city of Chicago.

Incidentally, after WWII, when my dad was allowed to leave the internment camps, he and many Japanese Americans of his generation relocated to the Chicago area. At the time, the Midwest was thought to be a more accepting and safer area of the country for Japanese Americans than the West Coast where most of his generation of young adults had been born and raised. He attended and graduated from the University of Illinois Urbana–Champaign and spent many years working as an engineer for Raytheon Technologies.

I've visited Chicago just twice before. Each time I'm here, my heart feels a squeeze, as I imagine my dad in his younger years, post–World War II, trying to break free of the emotional scars that he was left with following his internment.

Before I met Judy for lunch at an eatery known for its big brunch menu, I did a bit of online sleuthing. It was a happy surprise to discover that she was a dog trainer. I've always had a soft spot for anyone who can really connect with dogs.

Turns out, Judy and I have more in common than just our love for dogs. We're both moms, through birth and adoption—which kind of feels like sharing a secret language. There's a special understanding between us, because we know the unique challenges that come with blending adopted and biological kids in one family. Being an adoptee and an adoptive mom myself, I really valued swapping stories with her—especially about helping our adopted children navigate the complexities of their origins, and sometimes, connecting with their birth families.

I thought a lot about my own experiences of adoption and motherhood, and how what I've gone through has shaped my daughter's sense of who she is—contrasting with my son, who's never had to question his origins.

This trip has opened my eyes to how deeply adoption is woven into the fabric of so many families, like Nicole's in Albuquerque, whose life changed completely when her dad searched for his roots.

TABLE 39

There was a lingering poignancy to my morning with Judy. Back home, things were rough. My husband and I were facing hard times—and for the first time, I chose to travel without my wedding ring. It felt as risky and exposed as walking a high wire without a net. The ring now represented a great deal of pain. Wearing it had become a reminder of a toxic relationship rather than of the loving union it was meant to symbolize.

Seeing Judy's thirty-eight-year marriage—and watching her bask in the glow of retirement—really tugged at my heart. It reflected what my own future might hold if my husband and I could manage to mend things. I wasn't sure where we were headed, but Judy's story sparked a hope for the possibility of a settled, contented future.

Hearing about how Judy relished her retirement with her husband made me reconsider separating. I still loved the idea of growing old with someone I've grown up with. But I didn't want to allow myself to get caught up in that fantasy. I accepted the unfortunate reality: Instead of growing together, we had undeniably grown apart.

February 14, **2024**

Dear Diary,

Today marks a poignant milestone in my life: my first Valentine's Day in nearly three decades without my soon-to-be ex-husband. Ironically, I find myself in Nashville for a media appearance—a city brimming with the spirit of music and love. This evening, I'll visit the home of my dear friends Dana and Eric, and I will spend time with my friend Patti who is also visiting Music City. Dinner will be just Patti and me, and I'm surprisingly thrilled about it. My excited anticipation for Valentine's Day hasn't been this high since the early days with my husband—a telling revelation.

I toyed with the idea of reaching out to him today, to offer forgiveness—not to reconcile, but to forgive—as a Valentine's Day gift. Yet, I've decided it feels premature and somewhat forced. My emotions are still in flux—a testament to the complex process of unraveling almost thirty years of togetherness.

Curiosity recently led me to ask him what he thought my part was in our marriage's demise, a question sparked by a conversation with a man I recently went on a date with—a "meet and greet" as he termed it. Incidentally, our second date is set for Saturday, which he considers our "official" first date.

My ex, however, has left my question unanswered.

While my husband's struggles with alcohol and his actions at the end were obvious breaking points, I acknowledge my share in our downfall. Hindsight suggests we should've parted ways years ago—a sentiment he likely shares. Yet, we persevered, for better or for worse.

I hold onto hope that this next chapter will lead us both toward healthier lives. Perhaps by next Valentine's Day, we might find a new kind of bond as friends.

Wishing the world love,

Shari

TRAVEL LOG

August 10, 2023

Jennifer and me at Eno Vino Downtown Wine Bar and Bistro in Madison, Wisconsin

Table 40

Dinner at Eno Vino Downtown Wine Bar and Bistro Madison, Wisconsin

Jennifer
Thursday, August 10, 2023—5:00 PM CDT

Jennifer is a mom to two adult children. She was born and raised in Wisconsin. She is sixty-two years old and a practicing attorney.

It's been nearly two decades since I first met John, Jennifer's brother, at our children's Montessori preschool. When I posted on social media that I was looking for a connection in Wisconsin for my 50 States Project, John's response, suggesting his sister Jennifer, was a delightful surprise. She eagerly agreed to meet, which thrilled me.

My arrival in Madison was eye-opening. This attractive college town, with its waterfront and pristine downtown, stood out from other places I've visited. Jennifer chose a restaurant that overlooks the state's Capitol building—which seemed like the perfect backdrop for two attorneys like us to meet.

Jennifer, who has called Wisconsin home her entire life, finds her solace not in the urban streets, despite Madison's beauty, but in the wilderness—a passion nurtured by her family's love for road trips. This outlook sharply contrasts with my background, where such trips were a rarity. My singular camping experience, a comical mix-up about the meaning of car camping, still brings a smile to my face. I seriously assumed that when people said they were car camping, they were sleeping in their cars.

I loved the excitement evident on Jennifer's face as she shared her vivid tales of hiking. She was filled with exuberance as she spoke of her intention to traverse scenic trails in her retirement. Her zest has sparked in me a curiosity to explore the hiking paths of the Pacific Northwest—which is known to offer some of the most beautiful hiking areas on Earth. I was amazed that I have never explored them despite the fact that many of these trails are located in my own backyard.

I asked Jennifer how she celebrated her milestone sixtieth birthday. She shared that she embarked on a memorable hiking and camping journey with her brothers. Growing up without siblings, I used to pray every night for a brother or sister, so I'm always intrigued by the dynamics of sibling relationships. Conversations with women like Jennifer, and Kristin from Indiana—who are also close to their siblings—bring up my childhood longing for siblings. I'm guessing the odds are high that I have biological siblings, at least half-siblings, somewhere in the world. It would be a dream to find my biological family.

My stay in Wisconsin, though short, was filled with unforgettable moments. Madison's charm, encircled by four magnificent lakes, was breathtaking. Even in our brief encounter, I felt a fun connection with Jennifer. I was inspired by her independence and the way she is looking at her next stage of life—retirement—as a time to travel to magnificent hiking destinations for a chance to explore this wonderful world.

I took satisfaction in the fact that *retirement* has taken on a new meaning for our generation: an opportunity to embrace life fully rather than to slow down. Sounds like the perfect plan!

TRAVEL LOG

August 11, 2023

Beverly and me at Duck City Bistro in Davenport, Iowa

Table 41

Dinner at Duck City Bistro
Davenport, Iowa

Beverly
Friday, August 11, 2023—4:00 PM CDT

Beverly is fifty-four years old, married, and mom to three adult children. While she was born in Ohio, she was raised in New Mexico. She has also lived in Missouri, Oklahoma, Washington State, and Kansas. She has settled in Iowa, living here for nearly twenty years. She is an attorney who no longer actively practices law, although she keeps her foot in the legal field and maintains her license to practice.

Beverly was the first person I met in law school. I met her in 1992, just weeks before the school year began. She was working in the admissions office, I had signed up for a tour of the law school, and she was my guide. Beverly was in her last year of law school, incredibly friendly, beautiful, and easy to talk to. Upon seeing her tonight, I quickly noticed that all these qualities, which made her unforgettable, haven't been touched by the years.

In law school, Beverly rented a house with two other third-year law students, one with whom I was in a serious relationship, having dated him for two years. We laughed at the fact that although he was a nice guy, he and I would have been a terrible fit for one another in the long term. She and he struggled as roommates, as sharing a house together really challenged their friendship. We both recalled him having quite a limited palate—he ate spaghetti with red sauce several times a week—and that drove us crazy back when we were in our twenties. It's so funny to look back on it now.

You would think that she and I would have had a chance back then to get to know one another, since I dated her roommate. But Beverly, who was dating the man who became her husband, had a separate group of friends; and with us in different years of school, we saw each other only in passing. So, I was really looking forward to having the chance to sit down and finally get to know her. And I think she felt the same.

We decided to meet at my hotel because it had a rooftop bar with an expansive view of Davenport. After drinks there, we headed over to the restaurant Beverly had chosen: Duck City Bistro is a unique place where the chef presents the day's protein choices with a lively display in front of various cuts of meats and seafood.

I'm not sure if I ever knew that Beverly was adopted. She may have mentioned it in the past, but I had forgotten. I'm again struck by the number of women in my 50 States Project who are adopted, have adopted a child, or have a parent who is adopted. Beverly's mom, who was single and a practicing attorney, adopted as infants both Beverly and her older sister. Then, after marrying her dad, shortly before Beverly's first birthday, the newly married couple adopted two sons. Beverly was raised in a family of four kids—all four coming from different biological parents.

Like some of the other women in this project, Beverly has found her birth family. As I reflected on this, I realized that there are more women in this project who have been directly affected by adoption who have found their birth families than not—which definitely surprises me. Beverly's birth parents had passed before she had a chance to meet them, but she has found and met her half-siblings and extended family members.

I wondered if she had any sadness over the fact that she was not able to meet her birth parents. She answered kindly, "No. I think the timing was just right. I wasn't supposed to meet them." I use the word *kindly* to describe the way she responded, because there was no animosity or regret in her voice as she shared who she has met and who she wasn't able to meet.

When Beverly refers to timing, she is referring to God's timing. Her Christian faith is a very important part of her life. I shared with Beverly the anti–organized religion attitude that I've carried for many years. But this excursion across the United States has changed my views on faith and church. In particular, Christianity was always difficult for me to accept. I didn't feel comfortable with it because of the way I was exposed to it growing up. There was a lot of judgment, discipline, and hate. There was very little love and acceptance, which is what I'd like to believe being Christ-like is all about. Because of this unusual journey, I've been able to look at individuals and observe their beliefs—what church means to them personally. I can separate hypocrisy as a different beast—not as a blanket that covers the entire faith or every believer.

Beverly suggested I read the Bible. For the first time in a long time, that didn't sound like a bad idea. I'm curious. I found myself open to studying not just the Bible and Christianity but other religions as well. I decided that it may not be a bad idea to learn about different organized religions with the new perspective I now have.

It felt like Beverly came into my life once again as my guide—this time not to help me find my way through law school but as an instructor cheering me on as I carve my path through life.

As she would say: "God's timing is perfect."

August 12, **2023**

Dear Diary,

This year is a paradox—my best as well as my worst. I shouldn't label it the worst; it's more a year of profound growth and inevitable change. I sense that the Universe—or as Beverly from Iowa would insist, God—is urging me to embrace transformation. God seems to be almost shouting for my attention. I refer to God as *He* out of habit, even though I believe God transcends gender.

While in Iowa, I took a trip to the *Field of Dreams* movie set, and I had the best day. It was an uplifting experience, even in solitude. I met some of the kindest souls—including a local woman from Dyersville, the very town where *Field of Dreams* is set; and a man who shared photos of his treasured baseball memorabilia collection with me. My journey in Iowa continued with a live appearance on the *Paula Sands Live* daytime TV show in Davenport, where I felt warmly welcomed.

The friendly feeling here is so different from the angst I have begun to feel on my flights home to Seattle. I've been so incredibly lonely in my own home. I wish I could bottle up this hospitable warmth that I experienced in Iowa and bring it home with me.

Always reflecting,

Shari

TRAVEL LOG

September 5, 2023

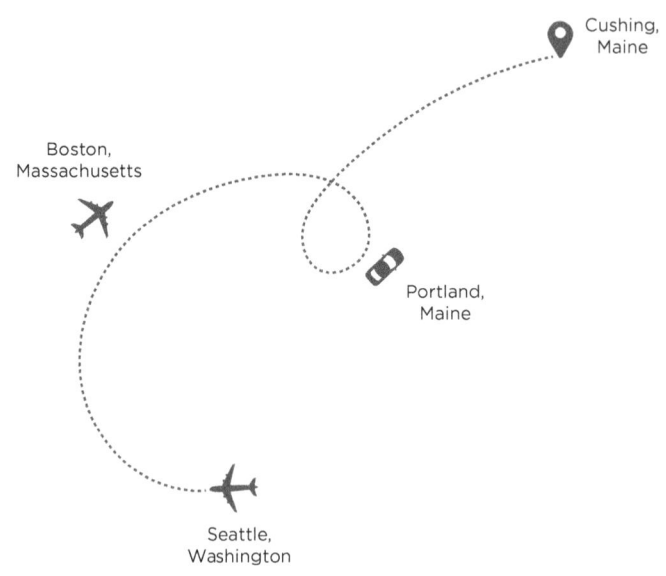

Cameron and me at her home in Cushing, Maine

Table 42

Lunch at Cameron's Home
Cushing, Maine

Cameron
Thursday, September 7, 2023—10:30 AM EDT

Cameron is forty-eight years old. She was born in Atlanta, Georgia, and raised near Jacksonville, Florida. She has been married for six years and has four stepchildren. Prior to purchasing a home in Maine in 2020, she lived in Virginia, and still maintains a home there. She is an attorney who—after working for twenty-three years as a lobbyist for large media corporations—became a business owner, writer, speaker, podcaster, and coach.

Cameron and I found each other through an online entrepreneurs' group led by the energetic life coach Susie Moore—who shows business minds how to shine in their own spotlight and how to be their own publicist. Our paths crossed when I dropped a message on the group's chat board about my quest to touch base in each of the fifty states, mentioning which states I still needed. Cameron chimed in, excited, sharing that she was from Maine and ready for a meetup!

Before our face-to-face, Cameron and I both ended up at a couple of media-pitching events in New York City. Even though we were at the same places, we exchanged only quick, courteous greetings. If we ever bump into each other again at some event, we'll definitely be sure to catch up more personally, picking up from our Maine adventure. But I am getting ahead of myself.

Cameron invited me to her lovely home in the picturesque small town of Cushing, Maine. As I drove up her long driveway, a sense of calm washed over me. The piece of land she and her husband own felt like a retreat—a little slice of heaven.

Cameron and I began our beautiful sunny afternoon together by sitting on her porch drinking iced tea. She shared with me that she recently waved goodbye to the corporate scene to pour her energy into her passion project, which she started four years back: coaching, writing, and speaking. She now does the work of guiding stepparents through the tricky experiences of the blended family life. She stepped into this world two years into being a stepmom herself, because she found a lack of helpful resources for her own journey.

Her dedication to solid, evidence-based practices has been the key to her growing success. With her network of experts, she has become a go-to guru in the stepfamily sphere. Cameron's influence spreads far and wide: She's the CEO of Stepfamily Solutions; co-owner of *Stepfamily Magazine*; co-founder of *The Stepmom Summit*; and host of *The Stepmom Diaries* podcast. She's also behind *This Custom Life*, aiding stepparents with tools and advice to smooth out family blending bumps. Not only that, she's a certified coach who created *The BLENDED Family Formula for Stepmom Success*, and she penned *The Stepmom's Gratitude Journal*.

Learning that Cameron and her husband had snagged their spot in Maine in 2020, not so long ago, surprised me. Listening to her, you'd think she was Maine–born and bred. I quizzed her about where home really was for her, considering her roots and the places she's lived. She laughed, and answered, "Everywhere. Everywhere feels like home."

Seeing how Cameron makes anywhere she lands feel like home really inspired me, since I was trying to figure out why my house no longer felt like

TABLE 42

home. Observing Cameron, I realized that she doesn't just create a cozy living space; she dives into community life—connecting with people, understanding their stories, and welcoming them into her life. She's a natural at joining, volunteering, and leading, making her presence warmly felt wherever she goes.

During my visit, Cameron gathered a remarkable group of women: Shannon from Louisiana; Sophia from California; Tyler, a Penobscot Tribe Native American (and the only true Maine local); Stephanie from Connecticut; and Ekhlas, who fled Sudan as a refugee to settle in Maine. Amidst the laughter and shared stories, I was moved by the serendipity of our amazingly diverse paths intersecting in Maine.

Reflecting on that enchanting afternoon, I admired the way Cameron perfectly exemplifies how to create a feeling of community anywhere. Her positive approach to life—building connections with exceptional gusto and fostering a real sense of belonging—left a lasting impression on me.

I felt a growing, desperate need to find a place that truly feels like home.

September 7, **2023**

Dear Diary,

Today, I find myself seriously pondering the concept of creating a home. It's a notion that's been on my mind lately, especially when I think about people like Cameron in Maine, who has an astonishing ability to find a sense of home wherever she happens to be. And then there's Cindy in South Carolina—how she felt like she'd found her home once she made a conscious decision to put down roots.

I can't help but wonder if this difficulty I've been facing in my marriage is somehow related to my own struggle with the idea of home. Have I been hesitant to establish real roots because I have been too afraid to do so? The concepts of commitment and permanence have always been daunting to me.

But then again, I wonder if having roots is actually necessary. I think about walking palms, those peculiar trees from Central and South America—the ones that move little by little to survive, always seeking sunlight and shade in an ever-changing landscape. It makes me question if I've been doing the same thing: constantly moving to try to survive, afraid to plant roots.

These questions are weighing heavily on my mind. I can't help but continue to try to wrap my head around what home is supposed to feel like.

Still thinking about home,

Shari

TRAVEL LOG

September 7, 2023

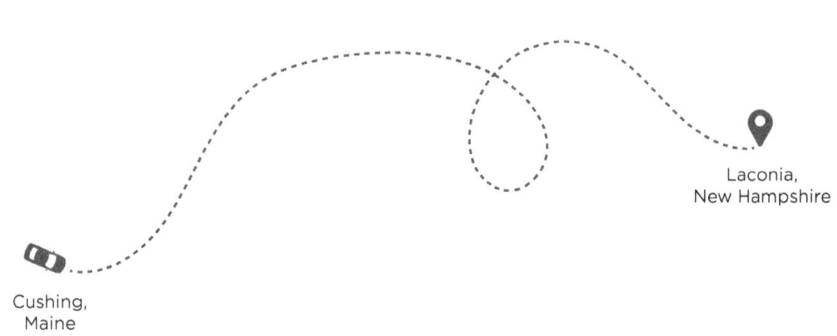

Emily and me at Wayfarer Coffee Roasters in Laconia, New Hampshire

Table 43

Coffee at Wayfarer Coffee Roasters
Laconia, New Hampshire

Emily
September 8, 2023—11:00 AM EDT

Emily is a forty-eight-year-old woman, born and raised in Laconia, New Hampshire. She has traveled and lived around the world. A few years ago, she made her way back to New Hampshire where she now resides. She has never married and has no kids. She is a speaker, writer, and life coach.

Finding Emily in New Hampshire was like unearthing hidden treasure. It wasn't luck that brought us together, but my determined search on LinkedIn for women business owners in the area who might be up for coffee with a stranger. Emily was just the person I was looking for—my needle in a haystack.

The coffee shop where we met mirrored the charm of Laconia itself—vibrant and inviting. It was one of those places that instantly feels like home, perfectly capturing the essence of New Hampshire's lively Summers and postcard-worthy Winters. To accompany our chat, we sipped locally roasted specialty coffees with our snack-sized maple-bacon waffles.

I learned that Emily's roots are deeply embedded here; her dad owned a local store, and her parents were the sort of folks who are always ready to lend a hand. No matter where she traveled, this town's spirit went with her.

As Emily recounted her adventures, I was all ears. Here she was, slightly younger than I, yet her experiences spanned more of the globe than most of us see in our entire lives. She talked about helping a child with autism in remote Alaska; she navigated the complexities of life in bustling cities like Istanbul and Prague during turbulent times. Emily's fearless heart and boundless compassion were unmistakable.

But what truly moved me wasn't just her travels—it was her commitment to helping vulnerable groups. She has not only volunteered to help children, she also spent years volunteering in a men's prison for a Quaker-designed program called Alternatives to Violence.

As I left the café, a thought Emily shared with me—a motto that she lives by—lingered in my mind: "You are not here to heal the world. You are here to love the world."

Emily's bold efforts *to love the world*—in communities across the globe where she has lived and worked—are inspiring. Heading to my next destination, I tried to wrap my head around how I, too—in my own small way, expressing the gifts I've been given—can best love the world.

TRAVEL LOG

September 8, 2023

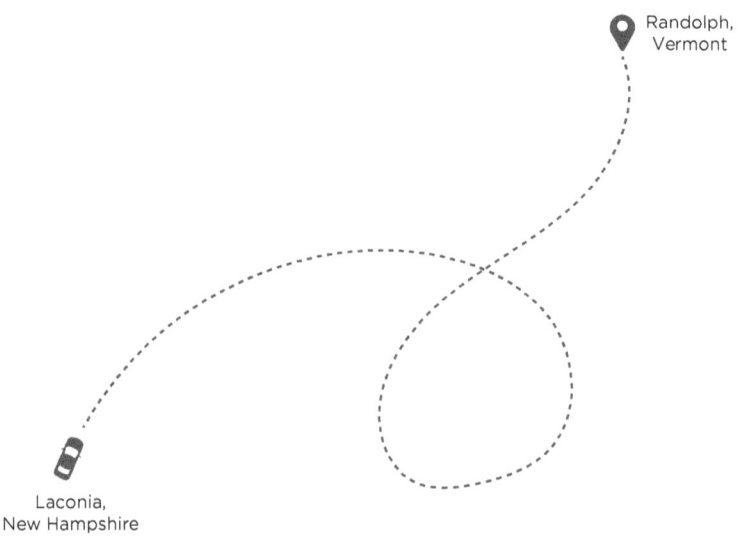

Kristin and me at Kuya's at One Main in Randolph, Vermont

Table 44

Dinner at Kuya's at One Main
Randolph, Vermont

Kristin
September 9, 2023—4:00 PM EDT

Kristin is sixty years old, born and raised in Maine. She has lived in different areas of the United States, including several years living on the West Coast. She now calls Vermont home. While she loves her current community, Maine will always be the place for her that feels like home—which she credits to fond childhood memories. Kristin is divorced, and mom to two adult children. She works as an attorney and a teacher.

I found out that Kristin and I shared the same law-school hallways, our academic careers overlapping—yet we'd never met until now. It makes me smile to think that we may have literally crossed paths before, without ever knowing it. I found my way into criminal prosecution upon graduating—more by chance than by choice. Kristin followed her course through law school with remarkable focus and determination—her fervor guiding her to the demanding realm of King County's prosecutor's office in Seattle, Washington.

My experience has taught me that when our paths cross with others, it is rarely a matter of simple coincidence. It's as if there's a grand design, orchestrating these meetings. Kristin's narrative, which she graciously shared with me, is a poignant example of this.

Just two years after graduating, Kristin faced a daunting challenge: prosecuting a murder case involving a thirteen-year-old boy being tried as an adult. Her intimate knowledge of the case, because she was the initial prosecutor in the juvenile hearing that led to his adult charges, made her appointment as co-counsel in the adult felony unit a strategic choice. As she detailed the trial, I was struck by the profound impact such court cases have—not just on the defendants, but on those who work tirelessly to prosecute and defend these intense cases.

Our conversation wove together tales of our past and present, delving into the profound impact our professional journeys have had on us. Listening to Kristin, I found echoes of my own time as a criminal prosecutor—moments that shaped my understanding of life's fragility and the importance of approaching every situation with grace and respect.

For instance, I remember as a prosecutor—when I was working in the family law division—there was a young father who owed back child support. If I remember correctly, he was a young man in his early twenties. Following the usual procedure, he was given a few days to pay his back child support or face jail (a system that is flawed in many ways). That evening, he killed himself by driving into a tree. I cut the news story out of our city newspaper and pinned it to my office bulletin board, as a reminder of how to treat people, including those I was assigned to prosecute.

Our visit to Kuya's at One Main coincided with a local bartending contest. The restaurant's popular bartender was in the running with her concocted drink called *The Bee's Knees*, which we both ordered. And, as if on cue, while we were chatting, a yellow bumble bee landed in my drink. A very Instagram-able moment.

Departing from my meeting with Kristin, I felt as if I were leaving a real friend—someone I could text at any time and know that she'd be there for me. In fact, I ended up doing just that, because I thought I'd lost my rental

TABLE 44

car key. I frantically texted her to see if I had accidentally dropped it into the little gift bag I'd given her.

Fortunately, my key had simply fallen out of my purse. When I went back, I found it near our table. I guess I just didn't want our fun to end. Kristin is, without a doubt, the bee's knees!

TRAVEL LOG

September 14, 2023

Allison and me at Flamingo A-Go-Go in New Orleans, Louisiana

Table 45

Brunch at Flamingo A-Go-Go
New Orleans, Louisiana

Allison
Saturday, September 16, 2023—11:00 AM CDT

Allison is forty-eight years old, and she has been married for thirteen years. She is part of an interracial couple: She is Black and her husband is Hispanic. They are proud parents of a son who is in his pre-teen years. Allison was born and raised in New Orleans. She currently works as a court reporter. We were connected through my media coach, Paula in Florida; years ago, Allison had worked with Paula's husband.

Having formerly worked as a newspaper reporter, Allison still carries that reporter's spark: She is bright-eyed and curious. And New Orleans—well, it has its own kind of magic, which only added to the energy Allison brought to our table. We sat outside at a lively Creole restaurant in the Warehouse District, within walking distance of my hotel. I decided to order a po'boy—a Louisiana classic sandwich—which was a first for me! And it was delicious!

As we got to talking, Allison shared something about her son that really struck me. There was a time, back when he was in first grade, that he came face to face with the ugliness of racism for the first time. He was at a party when another kid called him the n-word. He shared his experience on the ride home from the party. Allison, being the kind of mom she is, didn't just let it slide. She called the host, said they were coming back, and when they arrived, she made sure to have a talk with the offending kid and his parents, right then and there. Allison stood firm, making sure to educate not just her own child but the other children and adults who were there too—about the hurtful history behind that word, and the importance of empathy. She turned a really ugly moment into something teachable—into an opportunity to express compassion and foster understanding.

Hearing her story made me think back to when I witnessed my own kids face racism for the first time. It's heartbreaking, knowing a part of their innocence is stripped away in a moment like that. I felt for Allison's son, recognizing that this was one of those moments he'd carry with him forever.

After our chat, I wandered over to the National World War II Museum. I was there for almost three hours; leaving, I had a heavy feeling in my gut. Walking through those halls, seeing the artifacts, and hearing the stories—it's all a harsh reminder of the worst that humans can do to each other. It left me with a deep sadness. It pains me to witness so much senseless violence that is woven through our country's history.

But even with that heaviness, Allison's words stayed with me. She doesn't want her son to carry hate in his heart. And in a world that can be so cruel, that hope feels like a little light in the darkness.

TRAVEL LOG

September 20, 2023

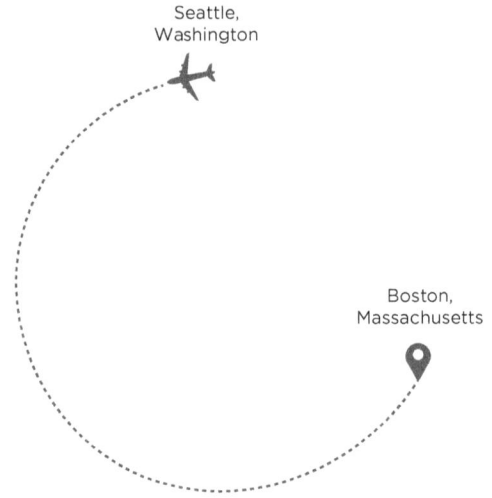

Tammy and me at Cheers on Beacon Street in Boston, Massachusetts

Table 46

Lunch at Cheers on Beacon Street
Boston, Massachusetts

Tammy
Thursday, September 21, 2023—11:00 AM EST

Tammy is sixty-four years old. She and her husband are Jewish, married for thirty-three years. She is mother to an adult daughter. Born and raised on Long Island, New York, she moved to Massachusetts for college, and has lived in the state ever since—calling Boston home for most of her adult life.

When I was invited to be a guest on Tammy's podcast, *Work From the Inside Out*—right after my second book *Make Your Mess Your Message* hit the shelves in 2022—it was one of those unexpected but perfectly timed connections. We kept in touch on LinkedIn, and as soon as I started piecing together my list for the 50 States Project, Tammy's name was at the top. Our meeting spot turned out to be Cheers in Boston—a place dripping with nostalgia for one of my favorite eighties TV shows.

The day we met was the perfect start to Fall, with Boston sunning us in a warm, golden light. I arrived at the restaurant early, so I wandered around and stumbled upon a replica of the *Cheers* bar upstairs. There I was, sitting next to a cardboard cutout of Norm, lost in the good old days, when Tammy found me. Her burst of laughter upon seeing me with Norm energized the room, kicking off an afternoon filled with easy conversation over lunch followed by a stroll through the splendor of Boston Common and the Public Gardens.

Despite being a decade apart in age, Tammy and I bonded over our shared dreams and the urgency we feel to make a significant impact by spreading joy and fulfillment. Tammy has an extensive background working with political figures and other leaders throughout her career. She recounted stories of powerful individuals, highlighting how they often exerted their influence simply due to their titles. We agreed on the importance of remaining humble and kind when granted such privilege.

We also discussed her family, including her husband's work with the Yiddish Book Center in Amherst, Massachusetts. This cultural institution is dedicated to preserving Yiddish books and the culture and history they represent. Our conversation, which touched on family history, world history, and current events, provided essential nourishment for my mind.

Before we wrapped up our conversation, Tammy reminded me: "We all put our pants on one leg at a time," underscoring both the simplicity and depth of our shared experiences.

Driving from Boston to Rhode Island, country artist Tim McGraw's *Humble and Kind* played on the radio—as if the Universe was nodding to our earlier discussion. The song's message about pride, humility, and helping others brought back Tammy's words about our common humanity and the small acts that connect us all.

Always, be humble and kind.

April 27, **2024**

Dear Diary,

Today is my daughter's twenty-fourth birthday! It's hard to believe I have a daughter in her mid-twenties now. Time flies. Next month, over Memorial Day weekend, the real birthday celebration will happen at a music festival in Napa, California. Lexi loves music, and I can't wait to share this experience with her.

Lexi is the musical one in our family. Sometimes I wonder if her birth family passed down that talent. It's amazing to see how passionate she is about music, so I'm excited to see her in her element.

This Napa music festival holds so many memories for me. My ex and I used to go every Memorial Day weekend. This year, though, I'm thrilled to be going with Lexi. She's a fantastic companion, and I bet this event will make for great mother-daughter bonding. It's possible that this will be the last year I attend the festival.

If the man I'm dating and I work out (the man who keeps surprising me in the best ways), I imagine we'll create new holiday weekend traditions together. But for now, I'm going to savor this special time with Lexi.

In the past, my ex would drink too much. There were even several times that I walked over a mile back to the hotel from the festival by myself at night. I'm looking forward to breaking that cycle this year. One thing I've decided is that I'm never going to watch a concert alone again. Too many times, not simply at this music festival but other venues as well, I would find myself alone watching the concert—with an empty seat next to me, my husband nowhere to be found.

Next month marks a fresh start at this event, and I'm excited for the new memories we'll make.

I'm cherishing this new phase of motherhood. Happy Birthday, Lexi!

Feeling some mom vibes,

Shari

TRAVEL LOG

September 22, 2023

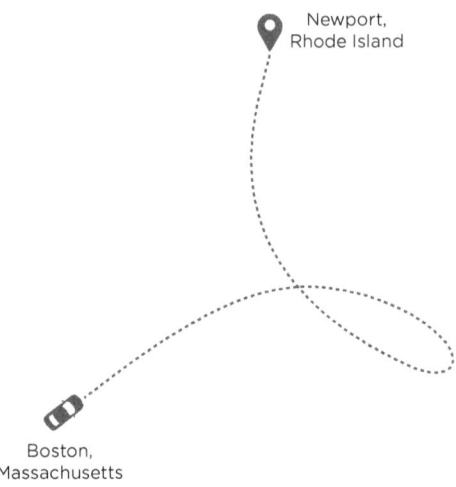

Sara and me at Brick Alley Pub & Restaurant in Newport, Rhode Island

Table 47

Dinner at Brick Alley Pub & Restaurant
Newport, Rhode Island

Sara
Friday, September 22, 2023—4:00 PM EST

Sara is sixty-four years old. She has been married for thirty-three years and she has three adult children. She was born in Ann Arbor, Michigan, and she's lived in several other states—but she has called Rhode Island home for over three decades. Sara was a stay-at-home mom; nowadays she works part-time at a children's boutique.

This was my first time in Newport, Rhode Island—a picturesque town that reminded me of Monterey, California. I felt a sort of magic in the air. It's the kind of place where you'd want to rent a cottage and lose yourself for a year—maybe to write, or just to discover the person you've become.

Sara and I connected through a mutual acquaintance—a woman I'd met in Seattle whom Sara had met in Copenhagen, Denmark, where her husband's career took them for a time. Initially, Sara agreed to meet me, thinking that our mutual colleague would be joining us. Once I explained that it was just me traveling by myself for the 50 States Project, she was unsure about going ahead with it. But her doubt was fortunately coupled with curiosity. I am grateful that in the end she chose to embrace our meeting.

We met at a popular pub located in the heart of the lively tourist area of Newport. We began with small talk, discussing what we'd like to order, and remarking on the fact that the place has been a standard in Newport for forty years.

Our conversation took a detour when I noticed Sara's arm splint. "My first," she said. I shared my litany of fractures—over a dozen tales of misadventures. I empathized with her as she shared how simple tasks had become battles. But her spirit was unbroken. She was returning to her part-time job at a local children's boutique—which I imagine was not easy to handle with her arm immobilized.

Beyond her splint, and my stories of injuries healed, it was her talk of plans with her husband to travel after he retires that gave me hope. She told me of her husband's flirtatious jests—even after thirty-three years of marriage—that offered me a glimpse into the secret to their enduring love. Hearing about her happy marriage whispered to me the significance of always making sure your spouse feels wanted and cherished, through every experience: the raising of children, the shared ups and downs, and the growth that comes from years spent together in partnership.

While my own marriage had its moments of testing, especially now, seeing Sara's unwavering spirit was like a beacon. Her candid admission that marriage isn't always a stroll in the park felt both comforting and real. As she put it: "Love is work, but it is work worth doing."

Sara's devotion isn't limited to her spouse. She chose to be a stay-at-home mom. Her bond with her three children, now adults, reflects the fruits of her dedication. Their recent travels as a family painted a picture of warmth, laughter, and deep connection.

Sara's words etched a lasting impression on my heart. It's fascinating how some conversations, even seemingly simple ones, have the power to stir the soul long after they've ended. I thought long and hard about the longevity of Sara's marriage—how the journey of love is paved with both trials and celebrations, with moments that test us and those that uplift us.

TABLE 47

In Sara's story, I saw the spirit of unwavering love—something I wanted to embrace in my current chapter of life. I decided that I wanted to invest fully in the people who matter most: my family.

I wondered, *Can my marriage be saved?* Will there come a day when, like Sara, I find myself telling a stranger about my thirty-three-year marriage, sharing stories of how my husband still flirts with me after all this time? I quietly asked myself, *Do I have anything more to give in my marriage?*

TRAVEL LOG

September 26, 2023

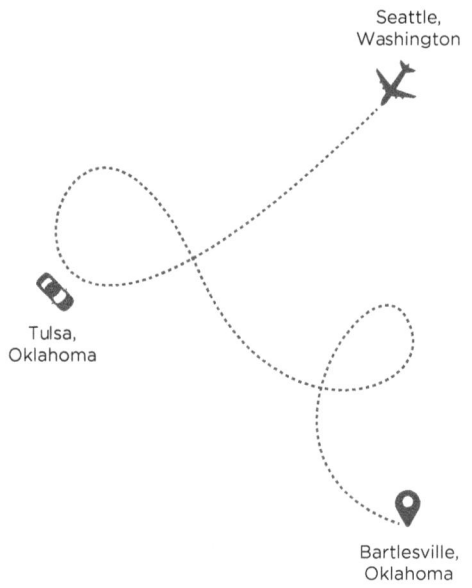

Janiece and me at Jude's Health and Java House in Bartlesville, Oklahoma

Table 48

Lunch at Jude's Health & Java House
Bartlesville, Oklahoma

Janiece
Wednesday, September 27, 2023—11:30 AM CDT

Janiece is thirty-seven years old, and mother to a young son. She has been married for five years. She was born in Wichita, Kansas. She moved with her family to Oklahoma at a young age, and continues to call Oklahoma home. She works for a global non-profit organization.

Before I even stepped foot in the door of Jude's Health & Java House to meet Janiece, I felt like I already knew her — at least a little. That morning, as part of my usual pre-meeting getting-to-know-you ritual, I scrolled through her Facebook page to make sure I would recognize her. My heart did a leap of joy when I saw that she knew American Sign Language (ASL)—a language that's been a part of my life since I was a kid, thanks to my dad who used it in his job teaching math to deaf college students.

Upon arriving at Bartlesville's go-to healthy eatery, I was greeted by the friendliest staff. Their faces lit up when I shared why I was there. They all knew Janiece, and assured me that I was about to meet "the kindest person in the world"!

And they were right. Janiece walked in with a warm, inviting smile, which put me at ease right away. We ordered and dove right in to our conversation, only pausing to take bites from our delicious sandwiches.

Janiece's stories, especially those about her college friends from an ASL class, felt familiar and heartwarming. She and her friends ended up as roommates and called their group "nerdy adorable." I smiled knowingly, cherishing the deep bonds and silent understandings that come from friends' shared experiences, especially those friendships that are formed during our formative years.

But it was Janiece's journey through health challenges that really touched me. From the time she was thirteen to sixteen, she faced three open-heart surgeries to correct an atrial septal defect—a condition usually found much earlier, and which in her case had been mistakenly diagnosed as asthma. Her calmness in sharing this—not seeking pity but simply presenting it as a chapter in her life—reminded me of Laura from Alabama, who was also born with a heart condition that required surgery. These personal stories remind me that no matter who we are, we all face tough challenges. And it is these trials that connect us, no matter what we look like on the outside or what families we're born into.

In those final moments before Janiece had to head back to her job at an international non-profit, I asked her why she had decided to meet me, a complete stranger. Her answer about the importance of connection and unity lifted my spirits even further. Considering her work, which focuses on reaching out worldwide to offer help and hope, her perspective wasn't surprising. It's a reminder of how even small gestures can have a global impact—starting from anywhere, including from the very heart of America.

As my journey was nearing its end, Janiece's warmth and openness, along with the wait staff's hospitable reception, reinforced what my 50 States Project has been showing me, time and time again: Friendly and welcoming people are everywhere in our country, ready to share moments of genuine connection, kindness, and love.

TRAVEL LOG

September 27, 2023

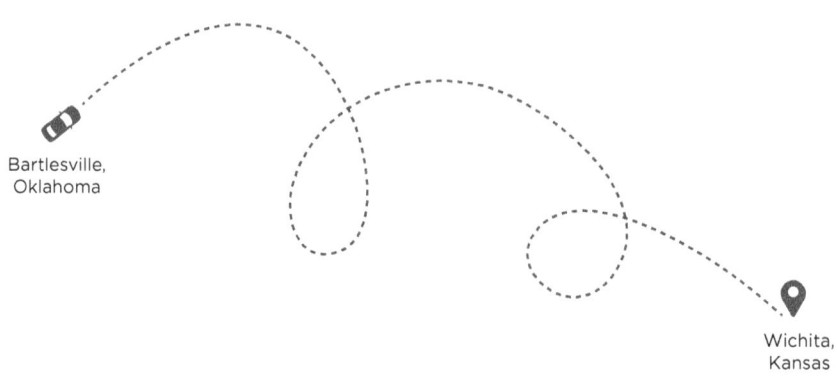

Jessica and me at Piatto Neapolitan Pizzeria in Wichita, Kansas

September 27, **2023**

Dear Diary,

With only two states to go, yesterday's experience was something straight out of a movie. I was driving my rented 4Runner—Texas plates and all—on an unfamiliar Kansas road, when suddenly I was surrounded by not one, but *four* black SUV sheriff's vehicles. My mind was racing. *Am I being mistaken for a suspect involved in some major crime? Was this vehicle part of a homicide?*

I saw through my rearview and side mirrors two deputies—hands near their firearms—approach my vehicle on both the driver's *and* the passenger side! Their tactic sent a wave of fear through me. Alarm bells were ringing in my head. I was terrified.

I told myself: *Keep your hands visible. Breathe. Look non-confrontational.* I figured if they were approaching me on both sides, they must think I have a weapon. I concluded: *They think I'm a dangerous person.*

What followed was a very awkward exchange. I fumbled with my phone while trying to access my insurance information via the app; I forgot my password for the app; and I could not locate my car-rental agreement, which I told them was probably in my trunk with my luggage. It all felt surreal.

This encounter heightened my awareness of my identity as a woman of color. Traveling alone, I'm always mindful of how my experience can differ based on race and gender. Initially, the conversation with the deputies was intimidating, but it became respectful—and even kind—toward the end.

They explained that I was traveling five miles over the speed limit. *A minor traffic offense*, I thought, which certainly didn't seem to warrant their initial response. I'll never know exactly what prompted their reaction, but I appreciate that the situation quickly deescalated.

Reflecting on this experience, I'm reminded of my conversation with Tammy in Boston about the impact of power. My interaction with Kansas law enforcement, though frightening at first, thankfully became a tale of respectful engagement.

Kansas will now remain a memorable part of my journey because of this incident—an obvious reminder of what a remarkable feat it actually is to be traveling across the United States alone as a middle-aged woman of color—often in places where there is no appreciable Asian American population. Throughout this journey, it was not uncommon for me to be the only Asian I'd see for days.

With gratitude,

Shari

Table 49

Dinner at Piatto Neapolitan Pizzeria
Wichita, Kansas

Jessica
Friday, September 29, 2023—at 6:00 PM CDT

Jessica is forty-three years old, born in Arizona. She moved from Washington State to Wichita, Kansas three years ago. She's single and has no children. She works as a brand strategist.

The September evening Jessica and I met in Wichita was hotter than a Fourth of July barbecue, with temperatures hanging out in the nineties like they had nowhere better to be. Jessica swore by the pizza place she had chosen—and let me tell you, it was the kind of pizza you dream about for days afterward. I even managed to eat an entire pizza by myself, which is something I'll brag about for a while.

Jessica and I have several mutual friends—all involved in some way with the fashion world. Vivian, the sweetest photographer you'll ever meet, was our mutual friend who connected us, gushing, "You just *have to* meet Jessica!" Knowing Vivian, I trusted that she would never steer me wrong. I knew I was in for a treat.

When we met, my 5'2" frame contrasted with her tall 6' graceful figure. It was the first thing I noticed. Standing next to Jessica felt like a paperback placed beside a hardcover. I couldn't help but laugh at our height difference, knowing we were going to be taking photos next to each other to capture the evening. Lucky for me, Jessica grinned alongside me as I set up my video camera. We decided to minimize our height differences by sitting down.

Jessica's love story is the kind that gives you a lasting smile. She and her boyfriend—known to each other on a dating app as *A Tall Drink of Water* and *Double Tall*—sounded to me like characters from a quirky rom-com. Too bad I didn't get to meet him.

Wichita was never on Jessica's radar as a place to call home. But love has a funny way of rerouting our plans. She told me about her initial fear of tornadoes—something I guess you'd better get used to if you are going to live in Kansas. Her boyfriend, being a local, was her calm in the midst of a storm—literally. He showed her that the storms we're afraid of aren't as bad when we face them together.

Eating that unforgettable pizza while talking about everything from finding love to dodging tornadoes made for a perfect evening. It reminded me of how experiences like storms and surprise pizza parties can bring us closer—making life extraordinary and fun. And really, isn't that what it's all about?

Cheers to finding storms easier to weather with friends—old and new!

March 19, **2024**

Dear Diary,

So, here I am, wide awake at 1:15 AM, which is kind of odd because I only fell asleep about an hour ago. But tonight's middle-of-the-night wake-up call wasn't about the usual divorce jitters or fretting over what comes next. When I think about it, worrying about the future seems a bit silly. Isn't the future, by definition, supposed to be a mystery?

What got me out of bed was this electric jolt of excitement—a real light bulb moment!

Remember Anna? The lady I met last year in Arizona? Well, this week I got to see her again, only this time in a cozy townhouse she's renting in Malibu, California. Her place in Arizona was a total inspiration for me, making me want to create a living space that screams *me*. And guess what? Her new pad in Malibu, though totally different, still perfectly captures her essence.

And just like that, before the crack of dawn, I'm hit with this wave of inspiration from Anna. She's got an artist's heart, a vibe that's nothing short of magnetic—so she reminds me of all the good stuff about myself that I tend to forget when I'm bogged down by all the things I can't lug around in life.

Seeing her so content in her new digs made me realize something huge: I'm not going to stress over how I'll manage financially with my new place anymore. It's going to be OK. More than OK. It's going to be *stunning*. Because that's just how it's going to be!

And my life? I'm choosing to let it be easy.

It's all about embracing everything life throws at me, and keeping my eyes on what really matters.

Feeling lighter,

Shari

TRAVEL LOG

September 29, 2023

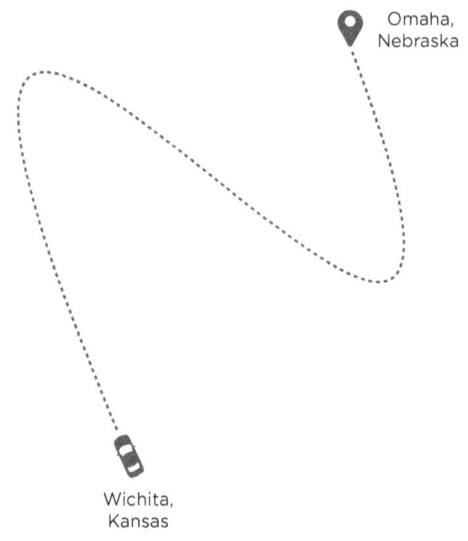

Sara and me at The Mill on Leavenworth in Omaha, Nebraska

Table 50

Coffee and Iced Tea at
The Mill on Leavenworth
Omaha, Nebraska

Sara
Saturday, September 30, 2023—2:00 PM CDT

Sara is forty-six years old, married for twenty-one years. She and her husband are the parents of three teen-aged children. She was born and raised in Omaha, Nebraska. She owns her own business, working as a social impact consultant.

Just about a month before I was due to visit Nebraska, the plans with my original contact fizzled out. No replies to my emails. Nothing. To meet this crisis, I did what has almost always worked for me: I reached out on social media, asking if anyone knew someone in Nebraska.

And just like that, Sara came into the picture, reminding me of how my journey started. Back at my very first state, New Mexico, when plans fell through, Nicole stepped in. Now, as my travels were coming to a close, I could celebrate the full circle this adventure had taken me. The Universe was nudging me, whispering to trust in the serendipity of connections.

Picture this: Sara and I were soon ensconced in a cozy corner of a bustling local coffee shop, diving deep into conversation that flowed as smoothly as the coffee. She had just launched her business, Ascend Advisory LLC. Sara embodies that entrepreneurial spark I so admire. Her LinkedIn title had caught my eye: *a social impact leader*. It turns out, Sara crafts strategies for her clients to amplify their positive societal impact—bridging organizations with shared goals while allowing them to stay true to their essence.

On the brink of a potential government shutdown, our conversation veered into how Sara's knack for fostering unity among diverse groups might be just what the country's leaders need. It struck me that her upbringing—deeply rooted in social consciousness thanks to her mom's ceaseless community involvement—significantly shaped her path. Sara shared that as a girl she would often accompany her mom to volunteer events. For her, it was simply a way of life.

Sara and her husband graciously invited me to attend a gala for a local non-profit organization they support, so I joined them later that evening. The gala for Autism Action Partnership was a testament to Sara and her husband's commitment to their community. The non-profit's mission of inclusion and prosperity for all felt particularly poignant given my grand journey.

Surrounded by a wonderful spirit of partnership and encouragement, it dawned on me that finishing up with this lovely event wasn't just the last of a long list of travels. It was a reaffirmation of the acceptance and belonging I've discovered and fostered all along the way.

Table 51

Home is where my next chapter begins. . . .

Epilogue

As I sit at my office desk in my new rental home—my Labrador Retrievers, Nitro and Thunder, sprawled comfortably on the floor next to me—I can't help but reflect on the extraordinary journey that has brought me here. *Table for 51* was born out of a simple idea: to break bread and break barriers. It started with a simple request to meet, which turned into fifty intimate and engaging conversations across a table—with the belief that sharing a meal could foster deeper connections.

The 50 States Project has blossomed into something far more significant than I ever imagined. Through it, I've seen firsthand the power of human connection. Strangers became friends, and each meal shared was a testament to the beauty of openness and the strength we find in unity.

Now, I'm preparing to give a TEDx Talk at TEDxEustis, which will be another milestone—a moment where I will stand before an audience and share the story of the 50 States Project and the Flip the Box movement that was born from it. Preparing to share my story—the highs and the lows—feels like a culmination of all the lessons learned from my travels across America. I'm reminded that vulnerability is not a weakness but a powerful tool for inspiring others.

I'd be remiss not to mention the loss of my twenty-six-year marriage, followed by the beginning of what is playing out to be a new experience of love—unexpected and beautiful—presenting me with yet another avenue of growth and understanding about who I am at my core.

This journey brought a sense of confidence I hadn't realized I was missing. Falling in love after an unexpected divorce—and simply enjoying the excitement of a new relationship, which comes with no expectations but only a curiosity and appreciation for the gifts of connection—encapsulates the feelings I've had throughout my travels across the United States.

The 50 States Project was not just a physical journey but an emotional and spiritual one. Each state, each person I met, added a new layer to my understanding of the world and myself. It was in the diverse landscapes and faces that I found pieces of myself I didn't know existed. The confidence that resulted from this adventure wasn't about being bold or fearless but about embracing my true self—with all my flaws and strengths.

Despite my humble beginnings and unknown birth family, I can still have roots—roots that I plant myself.

As I close this chapter, I am filled with gratitude. Gratitude for every person who joined me at the table, for every story shared, and for all the endless support and love. *Table for 51* is not just my story; it's a tapestry woven from the lives and experiences of so many wonderful people.

Thank you, dear reader, for being part of this outstanding journey. I encourage you to break bread, share stories, and build bridges. Here's to many more meals, many more conversations, and the endless possibilities that lie ahead.

And, by the way, this space that I now call home—this space that is a rental, which I don't own, the first time I haven't been a homeowner since I was twenty-seven years old—surprisingly it feels more like home than any other place I've lived in. I love it. Because it feels safe. And I've brought into it my spirit, my style, and my personality. Most importantly, I've held dinner parties and potlucks here, which has brought my friends into this space, filling it with joy.

I'm finally home.

With all my heart,

Shari

About the Author

SHARI LEID is a former litigator turned mindset and life coach, and the dynamic force behind An Imperfectly Perfect Life LLC. In her flourishing coaching practice, she specializes in guiding adults who feel trapped in stagnation, empowering them to sculpt the life of their dreams.

She is renowned as a friendship expert and professional speaker, and by the time this book is published, she will add TEDxEustis alum to her list of speaking credentials (February 2025).

Shari's insights reach far beyond individual coaching sessions. She is the author of *The Friendship Series* in three volumes: *The 50/50 Friendship Flow* (2020), *Make Your Mess Your Message* (2021), and *Ask Yourself This* (2022).

She's been interviewed on major television networks including ABC, NBC, CBS, FOX, and CTV, and she was profiled on the *Today Show*. She's written for and/or shared her expertise with *HuffPost*, *TIME*, *Real Simple*, *PureWow*, *AARP*, *Woman's World*, the *Toronto Sun*, and *Shondaland.com*.

After her extraordinary journey across all fifty states in 2023—in which she broke bread with fifty different women—Shari began the Flip the Box movement. This social movement encourages and inspires others to sit down with someone new, share a meal, and engage in conversation. By joining the Flip the Box movement, participants can demonstrate that they have the power to combat the epidemic of loneliness and unhappiness in the United States, and come together to foster a new sense of unity and community.

Contact

Coaching inquiries:
www.animperfectlyperfectlife.com

Join the private Facebook group, Flip the Box:
www.facebook.com/groups/558187349874133

Social media:

- @an_imperfectly_perfect_life
- Sharileidbiz
- Shari Leid (linkedin.com/in/shari-leid-51a53b10)
- @AnImperfectly
- @sharileid
- linktr.ee/animperfectlyperfectlife
- @ShariLeid
- *An Imperfectly Perfect Life—Life Unscripted: Navigating Divorce, Dating, Friendships, Careers, Family, and the Fifties*

TABLE FOR 51

For media inquiries contact Shari's publicist:
Kourtney Jason, President & Co-Founder
Pacific and Court, Book Publicity & Marketing
kourtney@pacificandcourt.com
tel. (917) 397-0140

For Speaking Engagements and Company Training,
contact Shari's Director of Development:
Nat Measley
nat@sharispeaks.com
302-690-1515

www.ingramcontent.com/pod-product-compliance
Lightning Source LLC
Chambersburg PA
CBHW050523100526
44581CB00002B/86